School and the Magic of Children

T0349477

Sara Miller McCune founded SAGE Publishing in 1965 to support the dissemination of usable knowledge and educate a global community. SAGE publishes more than 1000 journals and over 800 new books each year, spanning a wide range of subject areas. Our growing selection of library products includes archives, data, case studies and video. SAGE remains majority owned by our founder and after her lifetime will become owned by a charitable trust that secures the company's continued independence.

Los Angeles | London | New Delhi | Singapore | Washington DC | Melbourne

School and the Magic of Children

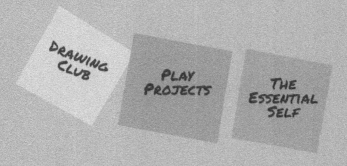

DRAWING CLUB

PLAY PROJECTS

THE ESSENTIAL SELF

Greg Bottrill

CORWIN

За Ива

Вятърът във ВЪРБИТЕ

A SAGE company
2455 Teller Road
Thousand Oaks, California 91320
(0800)233-9936
www.corwin.com

SAGE Publications Ltd
1 Oliver's Yard
55 City Road
London EC1Y 1SP

SAGE Publications India Pvt Ltd
B 1/I 1 Mohan Cooperative Industrial Area
Mathura Road
New Delhi 110 044

SAGE Publications Asia-Pacific Pte Ltd
3 Church Street
#10-04 Samsung Hub
Singapore 049483

Editor: Amy Thornton
Senior project editor: Chris Marke
Marketing Manager: Dilhara Attygalle
Cover design: Wendy Scott
Typeset by: C&M Digitals (P) Ltd, Chennai, India
Printed in the UK

© 2020 Greg Bottrill

First published in 2020

Library of Congress Control Number: 2019954903

British Library Cataloguing in Publication Data

ISBN 978-1-5297-0985-8
ISBN 978-1-5297-0984-1 (pbk)

At SAGE we take sustainability seriously. Most of our products are printed in the UK using responsibly sourced
papers and boards. When we print overseas we ensure sustainable papers are used as measured by the PREPS
grading system. We undertake an annual audit to monitor our sustainability.

CONTENTS

ABOUT THE AUTHOR

Greg is a writer, educationalist and experienced Early Years practitioner whose first book *Can I Go & Play Now*, published by Sage in 2018, explores the need for children to play and have an education that is done with them, not to them.

Based in Devon, Greg is passionate about the magic of children and the power of play, and is committed to supporting others to maximise early childhood experiences and ensure that children are given space to explore and go on a co-adventure.

When not busy with education or play, Greg finds time for his two dogs Bonnie and Eppie, and unearthing the joy in little things like woodland walking, listening to The Go-Betweens and daydreaming.

Discover more about Greg's pedagogy and belief in the magic of children at www.canigoandplaynow.com

'The bewitching song of the nightingale woke us up today . . .'

– Pungent Sun, Chai Khat

PART 1

THE ESSENTIAL SELF

CHAPTER 1

HEAD AND HEART

'Looks like another lonely Winter/Looks like another Winter's day . . . '

– Don't Send My Love, Film School

'Ah, Greg! How wonderful to see you! Let me just say how thrilled I am to see the children in Reception and Year 1 having an opportunity to play. It's fantastic to see all the great Early Years practice that I learned about during my teacher training living and breathing in my own school.

'Isn't it wonderful how the entire school leadership team is on board with your pedagogy and agree that a "book scrutiny" is entirely inappropriate practice to bring to young children because it makes the children feel like the only time writing has value is if it's in a book? The more I think about it, the more I see that there is a power in the way that you are enabling the children to find space for themselves as well as achieving the outcomes we expect as adults.

'I've been thinking recently that I'd like you to run a series of staff meetings every Wednesday after school to demonstrate to the rest of the school team just how important emotional connection and joy truly are. Why not plan six weeks' worth of CPD – that should give ample time to explore it all, and if that's not enough time, we can always add more since I know that Early Years practice is critical for the rest of the school to understand and try to implement. I've another great idea – why don't we follow your lead and do away with photocopiable sheets, and when we do science and maths and writing, let's encourage everyone to get outside or have some freedoms to explore their own thinking and fascinations.

'I completely get it that most of what we have been doing in this school is a mere illusion of learning. The other day, I was in Year 5 and although everyone was quiet and sitting at a table with their heads down, I knew that there were very few of them that were actually truly engaged in what they were having to do – I could tell they were fully aware that they were only doing it because an adult told them. I also started questioning why the teaching assistant is always with Red Group and why I keep finding intervention groups going on with children when they should be doing P.E. or art or languages.

'Believe me when I say that I have seen the light and play is the way. I love coming into your classroom because I get the sense that children are engaged and making progress in ways that go beyond all the spreadsheets I keep insisting on. Maybe I need to question that too and begin looking at the children's names more to see how I can support them and get to know them better.

'Isn't it wonderful that as a school we can see how Early Years has so many lessons to teach us and share with us about the importance of hope and faith and love? In fact, the love I have found is like no other – each day is something magical and immersing myself in the magic of children has totally transformed the way I see children, how I see myself and how I see life. I can't thank you enough.

'Please, keep playing and playing hard. The children have come alive and all because of the magic you have revealed to me. Oh, how my heart sings when I am in the magic of children – I love play, I love how it unfolds children and how it creates the perfect conditions for learning. It feels like we can change education itself. It feels like we can transform our community and all because we all share a faith in children . . . '

Said hardly any Headteacher ever!

In fact, our experiences are often the exact opposite. We find ourselves in a landscape that wants justification, accountability, evidence, measurability for pretty much every second of every day. We seem to be confronted by a system that has no space for love or connection or the value of children but instead wants output, no matter what the cost. Output seems to be the Great Big All, regardless of whether it erodes children or makes them disappear completely. Preparation for the next year, for the next topic, the next lesson, no time to wait, just intervention, more homework, more after-school catch-ups, half-term revision sessions, more pressure, more talk-at-you, and all the while less space for the child, less time for love, less time for children to *be*.

In this book, I hope to share with you an alternative – a way of creating the conditions for you to go on an adventure with children. Education should not be a predetermined journey with map already drawn, with no ability to leave the path or pause. It should be a co-adventure. Child and adult intrigued together, sharing understanding, reciprocating each other, discovering joy and connection to the wonderful world around them: the world of nature, of mathematics, of thinking, of self-discovery and the joy that awaits if only we might have faith in the capability of children.

This co-adventure can only take place when we take the first step into the unknown. This can feel daunting and can open us up to questions and uncertainty. However, once we do take that first step, an adventure lies ahead like no other – an adventure so magical that it can and will change everything. And the reason that this adventure is so special is that it will take you into the very soul of children and of yourself.

In these pages, I offer you an invitation. The approach I am advocating comes from my soul to speak to yours. It is not didactic. What it offers is a way to take those first steps and then look ahead to go deeper and further into the magic of children. It is a way of maximising the skills that children can develop and give them richness that can follow them through school. It is an adventure through two worlds: the world of children and the world of Story. It is a way to create the conditions for the magic of children to thrive, to immerse them in the power of Story, for their souls to flourish and for the adventure to begin.

So, let's start and, like any great exploration, we need to prepare ourselves first.

Both Drawing Club and Play Projects have potential to transform, a transformation that our children deserve because children don't need the past. They need a future.

So, let's give them one . . .

CHAPTER 2

THE ROOTS OF LEARNING

'I don't know why you cut me up this way/Putting a cloud on my Saturday/ We're down a hole, we can't just stay/And decorate it tastefully . . . '

– *Dig Up*, Rolling Blackouts Coastal Fever

Is it just me or did anyone else think that back in the 1980s George Michael was married to either Pepsi or Shirlie, the backing singers in Wham? I had this image of them as a happily married couple travelling the world with Andrew Ridgeley (he would be married to the other one) playing to audiences, releasing hit after hit and generally being in love with one another. So, can you imagine my early teenage surprise to discover that, in actual fact, George Michael was gay? As was Elton John and Freddie Mercury (I used to think it was strange that he was often photographed with another man who looked exactly like him – I thought he just hung around with a body double in case anyone tried to assassinate him . . .), and Boy George and the drummer from Culture Club, and most if not all of Frankie Goes to Hollywood and Jimmy Somerville and Andy Bell and Neil Tennant – a whole world that seemed to be different and unnavigable.

And then there was one of my best friends, Richard. We'd drive round in his little red Austin Metro late at night down the country roads of Leicestershire, Pet Shop Boys and Erasure playing full blast, each song creating a soundtrack to teenage years under the Milky Way. And in later life, when we were in our twenties, Richard came to visit me and told me that he was gay. I remember giving him a massive hug and was so happy for him to have had the courage to tell me, because even then in the early 1990s it was a really difficult thing to do. And it explained so much of his struggle that I had witnessed growing up with him – it was a relief to have it in the open. And I still remember that hug. It was a hug of deep love, acknowledgement and of 'seeing' someone for who they truly are.

Fast forward to today and it might seem slightly ludicrous to have thought the things I did about the pop idols who were such a part of life. It might seem strange that it would take so long for me to see that Boy George didn't just dress up so that everyone would know he was the lead singer. And now if Richard and I were to be teenagers once more, I'd hope that it wouldn't take so long for us to have that hug.

And why do I mention all this? It's because slowly over time our cultural attitudes have evolved from the pattern of the past. There is, generally speaking, an increased sense that sexuality isn't fixed and shouldn't be feared, and instead should be celebrated and embraced. I'm not in any way saying that life is without prejudice, and I know that there are still many, many challenges ahead because what people fear they tend to bring their hate to, but there is more openness now, an awareness, a lack of surprise. My own children talk about gay friends as though it is nothing out of the ordinary, something that I, at a similar age, would never have done, perhaps.

And that, I believe, is the purpose of each new generation: to transform itself away from the ghosts of the past, away from the cultural norms that dominate and control us, and to seek new adventures, new ways of exploring life, not to blindly accept what has gone before but to challenge it, change it, eradicate the opinions and attitudes that restrain us from finding our own selves and our place in the world. There will be struggle, but struggle is the foundation of hope.

Ultimately, we need to find space. Space for collaboration, for dialogue, for a willingness to explore and change direction because to stay still is not an option. It requires a new map of consciousness, one that is based on three essential tenets: hope, faith and love. Hope that change can come. Faith that it will happen. And love that connects us each to the other in order to bring that change out of dreamtime and into reality. Without these, change and transformation, both inwardly and outwardly, can arguably never happen.

When we rise above accepted cultural norms, we become agents of change, we act. Every decision we make or is made for us is 'political', is telling us something about our place in the world. We plunge into the future through the present based on the past. It is what we do with our past that is so critical, whether we allow it to cripple us, control us, dominate our self-perception, or whether we learn from it, embrace it, and move forward with it, stronger and better armed for the future ahead or the current moment itself.

And there's one place in life where we spent an extraordinary amount of time, that is for many a test and a lesson that can take a lifetime to unlearn and recover from because it teaches us a subtle, yet not-so-subtle lesson about ourselves. And this place seems to cling to the past, refuses to exorcise the ghosts, is reluctant to have faith and is arguably removing itself further and further away from love with each year that passes. And that place begins with the letter 's' and rhymes with 'pool'. If you need another clue, you spent an inordinate amount of time there and you are very highly likely to still be rehabilitating yourself from it – yes, that's right: school.

Have you ever seen a ghost? I think I did once – in my house. A little girl with a petticoat on floated through my lounge. I'm 99 per cent sure I saw her. I hadn't been drinking; I was sober with a cup of tea. The air went really cold and then I saw her. I know it'll be hard to convince you because you have to experience yourself and I, too, have always been sceptical about people who claim to have these types of close encounters.

But what if I told you that ghosts are definitely real? What if I told you that you have a ghost inside you? A ghost from the past. A ghost that is also in every single person around you. A ghost that you can't exactly see but one that is present, nonetheless. It's a ghost that comes out from the past, the distant past, and reaches into you and walks with you everywhere you go. Its invisibility belies its power. Its subtlety is its strength. It was presented as something benevolent, but in fact it is the opposite. Because this ghost comes all the way from the nineteenth century and has its grip still all these years on.

It's the ghost of education. It's the ghost of schoolification. It's the ghost of control. And, unlike the ghosts of Dickensian Christmas, the message this ghost brings us is not to awaken us but to put us under a spell.

The origins of education lie in control, in authority: the Church seeking to influence and direct thinking towards itself, to have a society that could read the Bible and could be obedient. Feudal society, the rule of the father, of the figurehead, gave way to the authoritarianism of the Church with its structure and its message of sin and punishment for disobedience. To be a devout Christian, to practise goodness and submission to God's law was the route to salvation, and with the rise of Puritanism came the need to read. Schooling provided the perfect conditions, learning through rote, through submitting to a higher authority with punishment on Earth and reward in Heaven.

And, wouldn't you know, as the Church's influence within society began to fade, who should be there to step in? The State, ready and willing to control and conform children in preparation for the needs of the Industrial Age – work not play. As society became increasingly less rural and less dependent on agricultural economics, schooling provided the context for children to be coerced and brow-beaten in readiness for the factory. Children's innate ability and drive for exploration and to learn with freedom was slowly yet surely being replaced by servitude to the demands of profitability.

And this is the ghost that still haunts us. The ghost that is omnipresent. Its claws coming right out from the past. Children's natural ways of learning, through play, cooperation, exploration, self-direction being eroded: you have a lesson to learn and you are going to learn it. The Adult World in control, directing, instructing while children 'work' and produce, all the while slipping away from their true selves. We have a public education system that fails the public. The richness of what life might be, having time and space to listen to ourselves and those around us, to share our understanding, to playfully explore and adventure, children engaging in self-discovery, self-architecture, reconnecting to the natural world, spontaneous and full of joy, each day being The Best Day Ever.

Yet the Adult World offers the exact opposite: tests and four walls and homework and limited freedoms and instruction and direction and uniformity and worksheet and the Clock and mental ill-health and obesity and reward and Golden Time and Health and Safety, the tick-tock, tick-tock overseeing life as it erodes, a system that turns play somehow into a remote luxury, something that has to earned.

We've ended up like this because in the late 1970s we were offered something shiny and new.

CHAPTER 3

CONTROL, CONFORMITY, CURRICULUM

'Modernity has failed us . . .'

– *Love It If We Made It*, The 1975

Thatcher – the very name that growing up in the English East Midlands in the 70s and 80s was anathema. The mining communities decimated. Families and friends in the shadow of the coal mine turning on one another. Violence. Suspicion. Fear. The erosion of the unions and of swathes of communities, and replacing values and space for childhood into a race for possession and consumerism. We were sold a promise: a promise of freedom. Of home ownership. Of market forces. Of affordability. But it was all an illusion. In fact, Thatcher's Britain enslaved us. It introduced a furtive neoliberalism, bringing with it accountability, measurability and the altar of profit.

More cars, bigger TVs, double glazing, loft conversions, annual holidays in the sun, everything 'new and improved' – this was the Great Dream. Yet the size of your TV said nothing about you of any value; the new car with all its showroom shine parked in the drive said more about enslavement than freedom. Inexorably, we seemed to slip into an era in which objects had more value than anything else, that the internal world, the world of connection and solidarity, the world of imagination and of the self was no longer a place to explore because the objective world, of consumerism, was more immediate and desirable. So, this slow alienation from ourselves, from one another, from our work, took over life and the spell, the ghost from the past, settled over us and is still with us today.

And this ghost is very prevalent in many of our schools. Thatcher's bid to break the control of the teaching unions, to exert authority through the insistence of a National Curriculum wrestled autonomy, freedom and faith away from our schools, and in the void came accountability and measure, and over time the school business manager and the school inspectorate team came running over the hill rubbing their hands with glee.

And now we have educational systems around the world in the grip of spreadsheetism, in the lap of conformity, all the while holding the hand of profitability, leading children rather than creating a co-adventure. Children seem to be the last thing in the mind of the Adult World. Instead it's the outcome, cell F column 7, pink and green highlighters, bottom group, mastery, rapid progress, accelerated progress: all devoid of one thing that neoliberalism robbed us of: love.

Have you ever met someone who changes your life, who tips your whole world upside down, who you can't stop thinking about, who you dream about and want to be with every second of every day? Have you met someone who seems to consume all of you, all your time, all your brain space, who every song you hear, every film you watch seems to echo with their name? I hope you have. I hope you are with them now. It's this love that transforms us, that seems to take us out of time itself and brings great joy and pleasure to life. Bills, money, possessions, all the minutiae of daily living, of consumerism, of the story we've been told – that to be a good consumer is to live – loses its veneer and there in front of us, like some bright ray from another planet love evaporates the ghosts.

And we were born for this. We were born to make sense of the world for ourselves, to seek connections, to find our own way, to discover ourselves, to discover that the world needs hope. That hope gives birth to faith, which in turn brings love into the world.

Yet the further we move into the neoliberalist dystopia of accountability, the further we move away from faith in children and the hope they bring and the love that we hold for them. There's a lyric by the Australian band, The Go-Betweens: '*Why do people who read Dostoevsky look like Dostoevsky . . . ?*' and I often think the same about education: '*Why do people who never play look like they never play . . . ?*'

There is no love in a spreadsheet cell. There can be no love in a worksheet. If you love someone, you set them free, and freedom is adventure and trust and growth. Control is not love. Fear is not love. Agenda is not love. The Adult World has objectified children on the road to measurability.

The shining path with its infinite digressions and offshoots and cross-roads that childhood could and should be on has gone dim and instead been replaced by a road well-trodden, each child led, with little considera-tion for joy, as though on an airport travellator, soulless, functional and one-dimensional.

CHAPTER 4

THE ILLUSION OF LEARNING

'And I'll just sit and wonder why/It's just a foreign town with a foreign mind/ Why is everything so cut and dry?'

– *Gentlemen Take Polaroids*, Japan

The ghost of the past is holding hands with something. Something spell-like. Something that is equally as malevolent and damaging, and yet we take it as normal. It's the illusion of learning.

The illusion of learning is the paradigm we have created that we have come to believe makes 'education' education. They are the Adult World systems that we impose on children because we have always done them. We had them done to us. Previous generations had them done to them, and we do them to the children in front of us each and every year. We do them because arguably many of our teacher-training courses reveal them as right and proper. We repeat the past because we can't see it for the baggage it truly is. We repeat it because we haven't woken up to the critical need for children to have autonomy, choice and space within their learning.

We make conditions and routines and rules for children to follow so that they fit in with our Adult World view of what children should be: compliant to the Law. It creates reward charts and Golden Times and removes playtimes, and insists on homework and behaviour-management policies and time-out zones and school values displays and visits to the Head with good work in hand, and empty praise and lining up and quiet in assembly, and good sitting and traffic light systems, and Red Group and Blue Group and Middle Ability and extra maths and interventions, and on and on, and on . . .

And yet it's all an illusion, because children don't learn in this way. Well, they do learn but not what we think we are teaching them. The Adult World imposes a rule of law on children and on our teachers, and all this rule of law perpetuates the ghosts from the past, bringing them back from the grave over and over again.

And that's because the Adult World extends the concept of accountability on to children. It feeds them an impoverished diet and then expects them to feast. Yet it never seems to question the cook. It puts time and energy into TAs, interventions and parent meetings without turning the spotlight back on to the Adult World and its demands and its rules. It's like prescribing a pill without reflecting on its ingredients or, more importantly, its side effects.

The rules that Adult World makes move us further and further away from the love that we might hold for children. They overshadow the magic of children and all its wonderful possibilities. The Adult World view of education moves us further away from learning the more we insist on it.

And the biggest culprits are the illusions that the Adult World makes in the name of 'whole-school' policies. Two words, when put together, make my heart sink: 'book' and 'scrutiny'. It's aggressive, judgemental and sums up the neoliberalist agenda that threatens all that should be good in childhood and our schools. It reflects the lack of faith in teachers, it reinforces the idea that schools are run most effectively on conformity and, worst of all, it drives it straight out of KS2 into KS1, and then with a hop and a skip right into Early Years. We'll explore writing in further detail later in the book, but in summary a book scrutiny can only happen if writing is in books; it's my contention that the moment young children write in a book is the moment that writing dies before their very eyes.

So, there is a vicious circle – book scrutinies monitoring writing by insisting on writing in books, which in turn is devoid of all the goodness that writing can be, which is then monitored and gives way to more regular book scrutiny – all in the name of control and 'whole school'. A book scrutiny is a sure-fire way of switching children off from writing, especially when the green and pink highlighters come out too. The whole thing becomes one great big 'product' and outcome disconnecting children from themselves and the possibility that writing could actually be enjoyable and purposeful.

Another whole-schoolism that typifies the 'illusion of learning' is the Learning Walk – this unerringly regular visitation that expects displays and classrooms to share commonality and wall spaces adorned with word walls. Maths Challenges, Words of the Week, We Are Learning About, WALTs, WILFs, Our Topic, Star of the Week, etc., cramming each side of the classroom and the ceiling with an explosion of sensory and information overload. Our school leaders tick the boxes and move on, rarely considering the actual impact on the children who have to try to learn in these environments.

And our Early Years spaces are very rarely exempt, turned into a riot of letters, numbers, primary colours, laminated fish and footballs, bunting – the Adult World appeasing the Adult World. In turn, this gives way to Pinterest and the Facebook groups, the great feeders of the Adult World, where we 'like' what we see and recycle ideas in our own settings, all the while putting the children in front of us to one side because this kind of display has barely little to do with them.

The more we add to the classroom, the murkier we make it. In reality, less is actually more. Resources in hand before resources on walls. Tactile and collaborative before one-dimensional and distant. It's not a question of 'what', but more a question of 'how' – how can children access the information they, as a unique learner, need in that moment? The problem is that the Adult World can't measure that or make it into an object of accountability because if it's not clearly visible then it is blind to it.

I love a Behaviour Policy. I love the way the Adult World creates a document that makes children accountable from Reception to Year 6 to toe the line, to conform, to have space removed and to live up to expectations. There's nothing better than seeing children's names on red traffic lights in full view, there's nothing better than the shame it brings, the low self-esteem, the standing outside the Head's room, the removal of playtimes, the parent meetings, the 'could do better', the labels that we attach and the low self-esteem that we wrap up like a gift and hand over to children.

The Adult World is obsessed with control. We train our new teachers in behaviour management and seem to give little thought to the idea that maybe, just maybe, if we gave space to children, afforded them freedom to explore, to show them that life is about connection and love, not control and power, the Adult World could possibly spend more energy and time on nurturing the natural democracy of childhood and enabling thinkers and collaborators and doers and helpers, which in turn would reduce the need for behaviour management.

The Adult World focuses on restricting children, removing freedoms and choices and, in doing so, diminishes the possibility that they might learn responsibility for themselves and others through choice and experience, through mistakes and exploration, each moment providing context for them to see that their actions have outcomes. Children are more than capable of establishing their own boundaries and, by giving them freedoms to do so, we also communicate our trust in them, we show them that we have faith, that we can give them space to adventure. Children learn best when they sense, when they feel. When the Adult World imposes, when it fits a leash on children, when it decides and makes children feel culpable and to blame for not fitting in with the predetermined boundaries; it is operating outside of love, outside of connection.

The control we can have over the children, the loving control, comes when we give freedom. It seems counter-intuitive. The more space children have to see that they have autonomy yet responsibility towards one another because they feel it rather than because they have been instructed to be responsible, the more they are inclined to engage with their day. Children are highly skilled at democracy, they are capable of negotiating rules, of seeing the world from another's point of view, and of engaging in learning motivated by the means not ends as long as there is passion and purpose.

One example might be play fighting. The Adult World would probably do all it can to intervene and close down the opportunities for children to engage in this critical kind of role-play. Because this type of play lies outside the Adult World understanding or acceptance, it fails to see just how important it is – the rules and negotiations, the trust that children have in one another when they engage in it, the empathy towards each other, the way these types of games are flexible and contain all the elements of great storytelling with its characters, narratives, its improvising and thread of action. The Adult World is often blind to this, however, in the same way that it shuts down gun play with all its rich role-play, dialogue, and back and forth evolution of boundaries.

It's a bitter irony that most behaviour policies talk about the children's responsibilities, but hardly ever the Adult World's. It imposes without reflecting on the diet it gives them – the worksheets, the disconnection, the restrictions, the suppression of wilfulness, the classroom of tables, the play-grounds devoid of interest and with staff in a huddle, the 40-minute long assemblies, the minutes ticking away all sat on the carpet while adults blah, blah, blah. The ghost from the past. Nineteenth-centuryism in the room with its feet under the table, rubbing its hands with glee at the sight of the negation of children's will.

The Adult World needs to take a long look at itself to unveil what drives decisions around behaviour. If it strived to make each child's day more engaging, more meaningful, more about them, more about freedom and choice, then children could step into their experience with confidence and positivity with less imposition on the drive to learn. Because that is what children have: a desire to learn, to a-tune themselves with one another and the world in which they find themselves, a primal urge from the psyche to explore, to interact, to meet the world with self-determination and turn the world into anything that can be imagined.

When he was younger, my son Eli used to ask me whenever I said 'no' to a request whether I had thought about why I had said it. He asked me to give ten 'sustainable reasons' why I had said no. As it turned out, 'Because I said so' wasn't one of the ten sustainable reasons. Parenting in this way made me reflect on the rationale behind my boundaries, and what I quickly realised was that a spontaneous 'no' was control, while a carefully considered 'yes' was the giver of freedom and of love.

And this is what the Adult World needs to embrace: careful consideration. To shrug off the ghost of the past, the shadow of obedience, the spectre of conformity – this is what will transform the way we educate children in our mainstream. By doing this, we open up a system that can 'see' children for who they really are, and the moment we do that, the moment we expel the ghosts from the past and all that has gone before us, is the moment that the magic of children can reveal itself.

CHAPTER 5

PROGRAMMING CHILDREN

'You don't want to know me any more/Letting rain wash away my face/You don't want to know me any more/ Letting go of the inner space . . .'

– Inner Space, Chain Wallet

On my social media, I often use emojis of a 'child not robot' at the end of each post. It's a signal that the Adult World has to remember that it is involved with humanity and not with output. We'll explore the concept of humanness in subsequent chapters, but at this point it's worth thinking about what it means to be a robot and whether children should be treated as such.

Robots surround us in all walks of life from the dishwasher to the microwave, from the photocopier to the modern car. All are designed to complete tasks set by us unthinkingly, without question, without being able to perform any other function outside of those that they have been programmed to complete. Mechanised, fixed, directed and emotionless. The robots around us are there to enable us to find more time and to ease the process of output.

Do we ever wonder what life might be like for our dishwasher? Do we ever take a moment to consider what our central heating system must be going through each and every day to maintain the temperature of our home? No. We only truly consider these things when they fail or break down. Then we take more of an interest because at the moment of failure our lives change and become retrograde. The robots around us are on hand and have been programmed to enable life to happen.

So, it all comes back to programming, making a machine subservient to the will of the controller. We see ourselves as above robots, as superior, as the masters. We would possibly never consider ourselves as robots or the subjects of a programme.

If we were to go on an adventure, who would we choose to go with – a robot or a human? Robots follow instructions, are dependent, are empty of psyche, incapable of wonder or spontaneity. Humans, on the other hand, are curious, autonomous, alive and full of will to explore and discover. Humans can take risks not knowing what the outcome might be because there exist multiple outcomes potentially. A robot can merely choose the best option for the best outcome if it has been programmed to do so. It can only choose from the 'known' because the unknown is not part of its 'brain'.

Yet can we see that in our current educational landscape the Adult World is in danger of programming children as though they were robots? That they are dependent on the adult in the room to guide and 'teach' them, that they follow instructions without questioning, that they see themselves as empty – a culture of Un-think, Un-feel and Un-learn, contained and constricted.

Are we truly learning if we mimic, if we are held within predetermined parameters? Can we say that life is happening if children are living like shadow-selves, like pre-cut paper-chain men? What does it mean to truly educate a child? Is it to instruct and quell the natural state of children to comply, to see the world as we do?

Everything we do with children is programming them. We say to ourselves that we are not robots but, in many ways, we are – we tell children about the balance of power, their place within the world, among their peers, their family. Each and every word and action are a subtle yet powerful message to a child of their value and how they fit into the space that we create for them. We programme them.

We recognise the importance of 0-3 years for children, yet seem to forget that the decisions we make when they reach school age are equally as important. The Adult World bemoans children who don't fit into the prescribed ways of school. It hopes that these children's parents won't have any more children, then shrivels when they gleefully declare a few months later that they are expecting another child.

And the greatest danger in all of this is that it keeps resurrecting the ghosts of the past, replicating them, deepening them into the cultural consciousness. It keeps children within the known, within the outworn ways of schooling and is reluctant to open itself up to an unknown, to take self-determined actions without instruction, to experience the autonomy that we ourselves were denied.

This subtle programme removes choice and thrill and emotional connection. Globally, the average number of hours children spend in school each year is 779[1]. That's 779 hours of being programmed. Education is not about the test score. It's not about the school business manager. It's not about the Summer Holidays. It's about the programme that we give children and whether this values them within our society.

If we merely offer a programme that reflects the past, then we offer children finite possibilities. If, however, we open ourselves up to the potential of children and refract the infinite possibilities that in doing so presents, then the programming of children becomes something very different and transformative.

Parents are key here. We have to exorcise their ghosts as well as our own. They will be carrying baggage from the past, from their own experiences of school. They will be unwittingly handing down their own fears and feelings of failure around school based on their experiences.

It's why homework fails so often. It brings back memories for parents. It reminds them of the disconnection they felt to themselves and reaches into the safety of the home, and demands action and understanding that many lack. If we change the programme, however, if we begin to see that education offers us an opportunity to sprinkle extra magic over children rather than rob them of it, then inevitably parents take note. Their engagement increases and they start to see that school can be different, can offer something that will bring children alive. And in that moment, when a parent says, 'I wish school had been like this for me, I'd have done so much better', you know that you are beginning the journey of reprogramming the Adult World too.

As children go through schools, they are increasingly taught about growth mindset, how to go into the 'learning pit' and use strategies and thinking to come out the other side. It's a popular approach and one that may well be effective. I've often reflected, however, that this approach seems to put the emphasis on the children having a growth mindset rather than the Adult World.

It's as though the Adult World could do with a learning pit of their own, to see that the prescribed methodologies, giving children writing to 'do', maths worksheets, three-part lessons, whole-school lesson observation templates, labels such as 'mastery', evidence trails, teaching for output alone, afternoon interventions, termly parent meetings – the list goes on to create a programme based on the monitoring of outcomes, not the development of children.

It's the same Adult World that looks outwardly for blame. It blames the parents because they didn't do a good job. It blames the children because

---

[1]For more information about average time spent in primary classrooms visit http://helpmeinves tigate.com/education/2013/04/mapped-how-many-hours-do-children-spend-at-school-around-the-world/

they don't have a growth mindset. It blames the Early Years teachers because they didn't prepare the children well enough. It blames the rise of technology and mobile phones; it blames all the time, the Adult World looking at everything and everywhere other than at itself.

And the biggest problem in the programme the Adult World gives children currently is that there is one key ingredient missing – and that is a little thing called love.

CHAPTER 6

LOVE AND ARCHITECTURE

'And I'd float just like a paper balloon/If we could spend one afternoon/And disappear without a trace ...'

– July, At A Glance, Spinn

I was sorely tempted to quote the 1993 classic *What is Love?* by Haddaway at the start of this chapter. Well, I say 'classic' - along with *Love Is All Around* covered by Wet Wet Wet, *I Will Always Love You* by Whitney Houston and *Eternal Flame* by The Bangles, I'd argue that it needs to be consigned to the bin of musical history. A pretty good rule of thumb when it comes to deciding if a love song is terrible is to consider whether you've ever heard it played at a wedding.

Romantic love is a funny old thing, isn't it? We seem to fall in and out of it quite inexplicably. It can make life seem ecstatic and then just as quickly crush us into the dirt. I'm never quite sure when love begins, whether you can pinpoint a moment in time when it starts, but when it does, it transforms pretty much everything into one great fiction, one great swirling mass of magic that comes out of the ether. Every little thing, every little moment seems as though you are living in a black-and-white French New Wave film from the 1960s directed by Jean-Luc Godard.

Some love lasts for a few weeks, some lasts a lifetime, but when it comes, it can come from nowhere and anywhere. Love changes our perception of time, our image of ourselves and the world around us. We become alive to the little things. We enter into some kind of resurrection of the self, a rebirth accepting someone else's otherness and taking it into our very bones, our hearts. There is no better place to get lost in than to be lost in love – and I'm not talking about the kind of saccharine love you read about on a Valentine's card. I'm talking about the kind of love that doesn't want to possess or control, but instead gives freedom and space for the one you love to grow and emerge not because of you, but because of themselves, and the more they do this, the more love you feel.

And the heart and freedom are equally as important when it comes to children. When we love children, we give them freedom. When we love children, we abdicate power over them. Love comes from faith. When we have faith in children, when we loosen the binds that come from the ghosts of the past, then we show children that we love them, that we trust them, that they have a power, not the power of love, but the power of self, the power to have autonomy, to wonder, to question, to explore and to find new possibilities that the ghosts of the past keep hidden and deny the very existence of, then we truly discover the meaning of what love is.

'Love Can Build A Bridge' is possibly the worst song of all time, especially when it was covered by Westlife, since they seemed to have the knack of sucking every last drop of passion or soul out of any song they got their hands on. Yet, the title is true. Love can build, and in an education context love can build a brain.

When we are loved, we wake up to our authentic self. To know love is to know oneself. More than any other emotion, love is eternal and makes us capable of achieving greatness.* It sets us on fire, and it does so because it does these things to us.

- It enables us to accept our self.
- It opens us up to new possibilities.
- It gives us the opportunity to embrace the unknown.
- It erodes the paradigms that we previously lived our lives by.
- It connects us to our wildness, our natural self.
- It immerses us in a dream.
- It transforms us and those around us.

So, when we love children enough to enable them to choose and to have freedom, and to immerse themselves in their learning, we are co-constructing the architecture of the brain. We become architects alongside children in the moment of interaction, no longer educators alone, but co-constructors of psyche and the very self. If we retain the fixed notion that the adult is the holder of knowledge, is the controller of 'no', is the point of reference for children's experience, then we diminish the possibility that children might see themselves in a new way, a way in which they can see themselves as autonomous and capable and confident, all the things that the ghosts of the past deny us.

Children do need adults, however. We aren't offering them complete freedom. They need us to challenge their thinking, show new paths, suggest approaches that they may not have considered, prompt them to think more deeply and sprinkle our own magic and new skills over their experiences. Children need connection – with one another and with adults also. Their sense of belonging has two strands: belonging to themselves and belonging to a cultural environment. Children's understanding evolves with our expert interactions when they need them, when their self-direction takes them to a point at which we can enable them to go further and deeper – they need our wisdom at times. But this doesn't necessarily always need to inhibit freedom, choice, creativity or erode their self-confidence. This skilful interplay is possibly one of the hardest things to get right – it's like a dance that both partners need to learn just by feeling the rhythm and movement of one another.

This interplay is a little like kite surfing. The stronger you grip, the more the kite will pull on you and afford you less control. The lighter your touch, then the more responsive the kite will become. In the same way, children need the lightness of fingertip-touch interactions.

Just as an aside, love can also be incredibly debilitating and leave you shattered into a million pieces and you feel like you never want to live another second, and all you want to do is lie in bed and listen to The Cure over and over and never go outside, and eat ice cream all day, and cry a lot and wish you'd never been born, and that you'll never love ever again, and love is stupid and why would anyone ever want to fall in love, and you spend tons of time thinking about the person who doesn't love you either in the first place or used to and you just can't stop and neither will the pain, and it goes on and on and on . . . until you meet someone else. And then you seem to forget and do it all over again.

CHAPTER 7

A NEW SOUL: THE ESSENTIAL SELF

'Do you think it's time for us to go?/Start a different life/One where we can grow?'

– After You, Plastic Picnic

Have you met your soul mate? Someone who echoes you? Fulfils you? Seems to be made from the same atoms as you, mirrors you, challenges you, inspires you to greater things and to be the 'real' you? A soul mate can be a friend, a lover or even a sibling. Maybe there is more than one soul mate for each of us. Maybe you haven't met them yet. A soul mate is some-one who we all seem to believe is out there somewhere.

The word 'soul' is vital to our understanding of children and education. A soul is the unique nature of being. It is energy inside us. It is our 'alive-ness', our psyche. And Early Years and all the education that follows it should be jam-packed with soul.

The soul and its formation, its moulding, its 'shapeness' emerges from how children make sense of the world in which they find themselves. To make sense of the world, they need to make sense of themselves. They need to make sense of their otherness and the otherness of the culture they find themselves in; they need to make sense of place and their role within it.

A soul is something that awaits to be unfolded. The child's mind, their eyes on the world, their dream and their daydreams all combine to take form. Children want and need to be seen, to be heard, to be present and to 'exist'. It is the Adult World's responsibility, then, to create the conditions and the landscape, to rearrange their own thinking and self-image, to ensure that children can reveal themselves.

Education then becomes an act of 'soulification', adults and children interacting and exploring so that both can find the shape to their true natures. Because by letting go of control, by adventuring with children, the Adult World soulifies itself too, reveals new ways of thinking and seeing the world. To soulify children is to refuse to give up on the desire for the future. It turns us into co-constructors of knowledge so that life and experience can be anything we can imagine. We enter the democracy of childhood when we let go of the need to control. This can be alarming for adults. It can be a threat to our perceived role, but when we see the soul of children, we come alive ourselves. We begin to rewrite our own story of who we are and our place in the world, no longer the holders of power but the co-creators of connection, exploration, growth and joy.

Soul imagines what 'could be', not what already is. Soul is a force of creativity both of outward forms but also internally too. To create is to bring something new into the world: new thinking, new connections, new love, and each creation has the potential to transform something beyond the initial moment of its emergence.

And soul all comes back to the questions: What does it truly mean to live? What is life? What is our identity? What makes you, you? A standardised, monopolising, generic education system does not recognise the soul because it cannot measure it, it can't make it accountable, it can't test it or score it. So, it devalues it. It denies the energy of the unique child. It's why in England the Characteristics of Effective Learning seem to cease to have any role in the Adult World once children leave Reception. It is frequently negated and cast to one side in favour of the curriculum areas for which it holds schools to account – reading, writing and mathematics.

To truly flourish, the soul needs these three things:

- inspiration;
- vitality;
- acceptance.

It needs to be inspired by the environment in which it finds itself, inspired by the adults and the peers who interact with it and by itself by recognising its own power to change, to have responsibility, to self-direct.

A soul needs vitality, energy to explore and adventure within its immediate landscape, to be able to run and jump, and climb and crawl, to sing and dance, and talk and question and explain, all the while giving out energy while receiving it too. It's why the Adult World needs to bring its own vitality to the classroom, an energy that can never come when stood by the photocopier or planning for convenience. Children 'read' adults very well. If you don't believe and bring magic to them every day, then they won't either.

And a soul needs acceptance. It needs to be recognised and seen. It needs the connection to others so that it knows that the world is for them, that it is a place to collaborate and communicate with, that it is meaningful in its own present and will be in its future.

The soulification of children comes back to the concept of the Essential Self: what makes us truly human, because let's not forget that this is what children are – human.

In addition to these three elements, the Essential Self is made up of these attributes:

- a past;
- a present;
- a future;
- a voice;
- an ear;
- opportunity;
- possibility;
- exploration;
- imagination;
- connection;
- transformation;
- hope;
- faith;
- love;
- purpose.

The Essential Self lives on the knife-edge of the present with the certainty of the past behind it and the uncertainty of the future ahead of it. It is forever making sense from past experience to access the future as if it were in a continual act of awakening from what it imagines itself to be to become something newly transformed.

And it is the fact that when we let go of the past and we face uncertainty, the Adult World is driven to hold on to its control. It requires faith to let go. It takes faith to enable children to make the impossible possible. The Essential Self needs to be discovered for itself. It cannot be given to us. It has been shaped from within, through self-direction with the added holding of hands at key points along the way.

And it is at this point, if we accept that children have an Essential Self, a soul that we can take steps with in faith, that we can begin to soulify them.

We add to them, not erode them. We awaken them and ourselves to the index of possibilities that life could be. By soulifying children, we enable them to unfold themselves. By soulifying children, we give life because without a soul, what is life? Can life truly be lived without soul, without an identity that sings and seeks out new ways of creating and communicating and bringing change both personally and culturally?

We talk in the Adult World about children taking risks, about challenge. Yet it's the Adult World that needs to take the risks. It's the Adult World that needs to challenge itself. It's the Adult World that needs to go on an adventure as much as children do. The moment that we enable the self-architecture of children is the moment that we enable the self-architecture of ourselves. We exorcise the ghosts of the past and connect with the magic of children and our own internal magic, too.

When we provide inspiration, vitality and acceptance, when we recognise the Essential Self and all its beauty and potential, all its creativity and imagination, and all its possibilities to shape a new future, then we awaken. We engage in soulification, a thing more critical and imperative than a spreadsheet can ever show.

When we finally pass away, when the death that is inside us finally claims us, what will our echo be? What legacy do we leave? Do we leave what always went before? Do we die with a large TV in the lounge, an expensive car in the drive and a second home in the South of France left behind? Or do we go knowing that we served something outside ourselves, that we enabled children to be the adults which the world truly needs? That we soulified children and in doing so soulified ourselves, so that whatever magic may lie ahead of us, we know that we left some of it behind.

CHAPTER 8

THE SPIRAL

'I don't want to waste it this time/And see fate as the end of me/I don't want to waste it my life/And know it was in front of me . . .'

– This Time, Land of Talk

The image of the Spiral is an ancient one. Its roots go back into the age of magic and is considered by many cultures to be a sacred symbol. It represents 'journey', the voyage of change through life. We pass through the Spiral, evolving and transforming as we do so, a vortex of energy and consciousness, a pilgrimage towards self-realisation. It represents the adventure of the soul.

Our own culture attempts to define this journey for us: it hands us ideas of morality, of success, of what we should pursue. It offers us TV shows and iPads, and holidays and cars and houses, and 'teaches' us to aspire to wealth and betterment. Most Western cultures look outwards – we become delineated by our possessions, by the things we have around us. And, yet, we remain poor because this isn't life. This isn't success. The inner world is what truly defines us – this is our 'who-ness'. We travel though the Spiral as a 'who'. The Spiral is the journey of the soul, of the self.

There is a flow within the Spiral. It is a constant stream of life, each moment an unfolding, a revealing of ourselves. The Spiral is our energy, our identity, our self-architecture. To travel through the Spiral we need autonomy counterpointed by solidarity. We need a vision of who we are and who we are with others. We need to dream, to imagine, to explore. It is how we make sense of the world – an infinite dream of the soul. The soul both shapes itself and is shaped by those around us, all the while being pushed forward by Time.

Every second that we spend in the Spiral is a second of life. Every second is an opportunity, a possibility. Time pushes us into the future, into who our future selves will be. The decisions we make and those that are made for us are inextricably linked, moulding us from the present towards the future. If this is the case, then every second is precious. Every opportunity to seize life and its richness should be taken. For what is life other than to live and live as fully as we can? And if that is the case, then what shape does our education system try to impose on us? Does it enable us while we are within it to live life fully – with joy and with a sense of adventure?

Because education systems are sycophantic and increasingly inward-looking, the flow of what life could be for young children is nullified. What should be flow and growth of self is blocked and controlled and replaced – it acts like a dam against the tide of life. It denies the adventure and offers a predetermined journey, each second within it going to waste, negating energy, stunting the possibilities that life could be.

Do we live if we can only mimic, if we exist within predetermined parameters? Can we say that life is fully happening if we live a pre-cut shadow self? Does life not need soul? Are we 'being' if we are living how we are made to live? To truly adventure through the Spiral we need risk, discovery, collaborations, curiosity, the ability to take on the unknown, confidence and a strong sense of self – all the things that play gives children and then school slowly erodes.

It's as though when we finally emerge from the school system we have to rehabilitate ourselves to then continue through the Spiral. We have to learn to live again, we have to learn independence and find ourselves because we have spent fourteen years having our energy blocked, our essential selves eroded.

All the attributes that we once possessed, all the potential that we had when we first entered the world have to be refound. We have to go on a new journey of self-discovery. Fourteen precious years have been taken from us. The Adult World has its gradings, its spreadsheets and their accolades, but what of the children who are now confronted by a world that needs soul?

It's as though the Adult World fears the energy of children. It has to have compliance. It has to have control. Yet the control prevents the unfolding of children. It blocks all the possibilities that life could be. And yet there's no way of getting off the Spiral, because the Spiral is life, Time pushing us away from the school gate towards responsibility and Adult Worldism.

Yet how different could all this be if we only took the risk to adventure with children? How different might the future be if we saw education as part of the richness of life, not something to survive or to get through, but instead something that embraces the essential self and enables life to be lived to its fullest. Isn't that the lesson that education should truly teach? That we have energy, we have ideas, we have the strength and bravery to face what lies ahead in the Spiral as we pass through it.

If we subjugate and control children, then we are replacing their potential with authority, and the authority of school ends at eighteen. What, then, in life? Whose authority do we turn to? Who will help us? If we have been eroded through school, we have lost the ability to help ourselves.

The Adult World has created these stop/start points in life that we have to emerge from and into. But if it has eroded children to the point that they live in fear of their own once great potential, if they no longer have a strong sense of self with which to go out into the world and confront the malevolence and the unknown in the rest of the Spiral, then we have cheated them of what life could have been.

It's why we have to resist the top-down pressures of 'school-readiness' and wholeschoolism, because these stem from forces that are not based in love. And in Early Years we have the ability to enable children to unfold all the strength they will possibly need. We have to push back because what is at stake is bigger than education.

The Spiral is ultimately a story, a story that we write for ourselves and in some senses with one another. The responsibility of education doesn't start with itself or business or society. It starts with the individual, with the unique beingness of life.

Education has to transform itself into the co-adventure, into the researcher of the soul and all its infinite possibility – it's only then that life can truly be lived, not coped with, not struggled through, but lived and lived with love.

CHAPTER 9

CO-RESEARCHING, CO-ADVENTURING AND THE IMPORTANCE OF INTRIGUE

'I've been looking so long at my pictures of you/That I almost believe that they're real . . .'

– Pictures Of You, The Cure

Yesterday, for the first time in my life, I found myself on a railway platform taking a video of an old locomotive train as it passed through the station. Something inside me told me to video it, as if it was something special, an important moment – except it wasn't, of course. I ended up with a poorly shot ten-second clip of a flash of steam, some old carriages and lots of noise, and then it was gone. There in that moment, I found myself shamefully trainspotting.

It's an obsession for many people. Standing on cold railway platforms, video camera in hand, recording the passing of trains on their way through, noting the engine numbers, ticking them off. Typically, it's middle-aged men and they tend to be the object of ridicule – but now I've joined them albeit even briefly. I can see that rooted in humanity is a drive to collect, classify and order.

And so it is in Early Years. The inclination to use curriculum 'objectives' as some kind of ticking exercise. It's why we end up engineering situations and experiences in an attempt to prove and evidence that we have 'covered a curriculum'. It's yet another example of the illusion of learning. In England, we have Development Matters which seems to drive much of our Early Years provision, leading practitioners to spend hours hovering over children, iPads in hand, deliberately asking questions of children so that they can tick an objective.

Yet Development Matters is not statutory, and on the document it says very clearly that it is not to be treated as a checklist. We teach children how to read and comprehend, but seem to ignore this very important sentence right in front of us for ourselves. Development Matters shows educators the typical developmental growth for children. It isn't the map, yet it is used as one, creating sub-bands of development, trying to 'force' children through them at times, so that we can show progress, spending hours painstakingly trying to fit them into and prove their belonging into Low, Middle and High.

Like trainspotting, it's an obsession. And, like train spotters standing on a platform, we are watching life go by while we are removed from the possibility of life that presents itself. When we go into children's experiences looking to tick something off, we are removed from the trueness of what lies before us. We get the soft balls out for children to catch, then tick it off; we go on Facebook forums asking how we can get more children to meet the standard for writing; we engineer and in doing so lose the authenticity and richness that children's magic presents to us. It keeps the control within the Adult World and it's why when you go into children's experience with clipboard and pencils, nine times out of ten you find yourself alone after two minutes – children aren't stupid. They know what you are trying to do, and over time they no longer 'believe' in you – you lose your genuine self and become a 'remote controller'.

It's a bit like those conversations you might have had with people who go on holiday abroad and say they have 'done' a country. They spent a fortnight in Croatia and then tick it off, going to great lengths to bore you with the details of some bar or restaurant that they went to night after night, and weren't the locals really funny, and, oh, the weather was so lovely and you really must go, and you'd never believe the price of a beer, and you should have been there, and it was hilarious when they went to the beach because there was a bar there and the barman didn't speak any English, so they had to point and, oh, it was so, so funny when blah, blah, blah, and now they've done Croatia, and next year they'll go somewhere else and do that because it's on the bucket list and, oh, is that the time? – they have to go, they have golf in the morning and they need sleep, but it's been lovely chatting to you and goodnight.

And not only does life come back to you when they finally leave, but also you know that there is no 'doing a country' in the same way that there is no doing a band of development. The landscape of childhood and all its magic can never be 'done'. It's too infinite to ever be encapsulated in a tick list. In a way, we need to see the Zen of Early Years, to see the emptiness that can then become something to discover. This emptiness tells us to expect the unexpected – it is the unexpected that should intrigue us and should drive our role as co-researchers.

Our research role can take four pathways.

To research the past

To discover our place in the history of educational thinking and our current landscape, familiarising ourselves with the ideas of Loris Malaguzzi, Friedrich Froebel, Maria Montessori, Peter Gray, Alfie Kohn, Suzanne Axelsson, Alistair Bryce-Clegg, Anna Ephgrave, Mine Conkbayir, Teacher Tom, Tom Shea, Nicki Buchan – the list goes on. It's about discovering the context in which we find ourselves and unveiling for ourselves those who are passionately advocating play and childhood.

To research childhood

To explore brain development, language acquisition, physical development, how we are shaped by experiences and conditioning – and all this can extend out away from the education section of the library and into poetry and psychology and mysticism and music and science fiction and art and music, because all are in a way researching and telling us something about the soul and what it means to make sense to the world and our place within it.

To research the moment before us

When we see ourselves as co-researchers, we open up the moments in front of our eyes. We see the exploration, the toying with ideas, the guessing, the wondering, the testing, the predicting, the making sense and the joy – all the things that we become closed to if we take control and engineer and dominate the space that we offer children.

To research the soul

Carl Jung said, 'Who looks outside dreams, who looks inside awakes . . . ' It's vital that we research ourselves, to discover our own intentions, our own image of the child, our own perceptions of our role with them. Once we know our passion and have a clear 'why' is the moment that we awake.

It all comes back to heart. It comes back to what is in your own soul and how you see children. If you have faith or are looking to discover it, then you have to put your specific checklist to one side and open up your mind to the possibilities that present themselves to you. The more you doubt, the more you bring a greater amount of the Adult World with you.

When we upcycle how we see ourselves and transform our role into that of co-researchers and co-adventurers, then we give space to children and embrace the 'I Test'. The I Test isn't a test of the children. It is a test of ourselves. It is a self-reflection on our role as educators and on the Adult World.

Inclination

Do we have faith in children? Do we see them as capable? Do we know that they are magic?

Intrigue

Do we want to unearth this magic? Do we want to discover more? Are we open to finding out more?

Interaction

Are we confident to enter the realm of children? Are we able to wait to be invited in? Are we able to have a connection with children that lets go of the need to control?

Invention

Are we able to observe and take time to see that opportunities will unfold before us? Are we open to giving children space and the opportunity to develop their learning through themselves and their peer-to-peer collaborations?

Imagination

Can we think like a child and see how they might develop the resources and continuous provision that we have offered them? Can we see that children are capable at planning in a way that goes far beyond how the Adult World might constrict learning?

Immersion

Do we give time for the children and ourselves to 'go deep', to lose ourselves in learning, to forget time and let our minds wander together?

Ignition

Do our interactions create in the children a desire to explore more? Are we able to question and tease out understanding, to challenge thinking and offer opportunities to extend ideas further? Do we create the conditions in which children are open to our role with them so that they are skilled at the cusp of their development?

Insight

Are we looking for and open to developing our own understanding of children's development? Are we gaining knowledge about the children in front of us and about ourselves? Have we learned something that will mean tomorrow has all the potential that it might have?

Impossibilities

And this brings us to the final 'I' – it's a trick one. If we have all the other 'I's in place, if we interact with children with a true faith and a real desire to gain knowledge of them and through them, then the 'I' and the 'M' drop away, leaving us with 'possibilities' – it's possibilities that can change how children experience school. It's possibilities that open the Adult World to being the co-adventurers. Without the I Test, we are like inspectors, controllers, clipboard and iPad bearers, disconnected from the children keeping them at arm's length.

Ultimately, it's about 'storytelling'. Are we going to tell the children's story for them or are we going to enable them to be the storytellers? Are we committed to empowering children to find their voice, to express themselves and their thinking? It comes back full circle to the concept of love. When we love, when we truly love someone, then we let go. We give freedom. We lovingly accept them for who they are and who they will become. And sometimes we have to love alongside, and at other times we have to love from a distance. Sometimes we have to hold hands; sometimes love is a message from far away.

Being with children is like being a bird. At times we are in the nest, attending and feeding, close by, reassuring, connecting. Sometimes we are far away, singing our song so that the other birds can sing in return and create the chorus. A bird cannot sing alone. Yet equally, we know that for little birds to flourish, they must leave the nest so they can take those first tentative wing flaps, totter to the edge and then fall, by themselves, and take flight into space, into the big blue, into adventure, into freedom. A little bird is born to sing and fly. So, with hope, with faith and with love, let's hear its song and watch it fly.

CHAPTER 10

PLAY: WHAT IS IT IN SCHOOL?

'I couldn't see you, so I had to run/Through the fields like when we were young/ And we lay there in the house you made/And we stayed there until Summer came . . .'

– *Wait For You,* City Riots

There are many definitions of 'play' – what it is, what it isn't, what it can never be. Trying to define play is perhaps like trying to catch the wind. Play, in a way, lies beyond adult understanding and arguably beyond adult involvement. We come up with phrases like 'free play' to describe it, and then there ensues much debate about the what, the how and the why.

For many of us, defining play means reaching back into our own pasts. We define it from our own experiences and the strongest memories that it provided us with.

What are your strongest childhood memories? What experiences do you recall that still echo with you, that if you think about them you are instantly taken back in time to a place where you were content and felt full of happiness?

When we think of these memories we often find that they are outdoors, there is a sense of freedom, there are usually other children alongside us either playing some kind of game with its own negotiated rules, its own canon of language, its own space and time in the world all around us.

Many childhood memories that we might recall involve dens or a special place like a group of trees, a patch of ground or some kind of hidden, secret and clandestine little hidey-hole. If you look at the illustrations of Shirley Hughes, almost all of them tell us of the sense of freedom that children seem to find in enclosed spaces, a Tardis-like cosiness that opens up the possibilities of imagination and dream. It's as though these powerful memories are centred around escape and being able to autonomously find meaning in experience.

Or it's a memory of being with other children, running, jumping, climbing, exploring, discovering seemingly long-forgotten spaces that can be the Adventure of Anything, a world within a world within a world, where wildness and connection, both to one another and to nature, stir something deep within us so that we feel that we are made of light and the summer lies before us, a landscape whose horizon is infinite and immeasurable. It's these moments in which we are arguably truly playing. We are lost to time, we are in the Dreamtime: we are in the world, but at the same time the world is in us. We are *being*.

There are typically two things absent in much of our strongest childhood memories: the first is a curriculum. The second is the presence of adults. Schools have both, however, so the biggest question is possibly this: 'Can children ever really play in school? Can children ever to be truly playing if there are adults present, if there are rules and a curriculum?'

If we define play as being free and only happening in the absence of adults, then in some ways we make a rationale for schools not to embrace it, since it becomes something that schools cannot provide, thus cementing the formality and controlled experiences. If we do that, then nothing changes, and the ghosts of the past remain alive and well. We continue to sideline play and dismiss it as frivolous and not critical to learning.

And yet, play is absolutely essential to learning because it *is* learning. It is the way that children make sense of the world and themselves, and it offers us a richness that we should strive to get as close to as we can. The elements of play – of risk, of exploration, of curiosity, of wonder, of choice – can all be present in our classrooms; it may not be 'pure play', but a strong and living echo of play is better than none at all.

It's as though we need to create a new vocabulary for the kind of school experience that we might give children. The best I can come up with is 'plearning' – a combination of play and learning, which in turn creates these words:

Plelf – play self – the discovery and expression of the self through play.

Plue – play glue – the connections that we make and embed by playing.

Ploy – play joy – the deep emotional response we have when we play.

Plange – play change - the transformation that we see when children engage in play.

So perhaps in a school context, we can aim towards an echo of play, an echo that involves physicality, exploration, wonder, self-direction, collaboration and choice – and all these come about when we loosen control over experience. The Adult World does not have to be about conformity. It does not have to be about delivery and test and worksheet and sit-here-do-this-now-go-over-there-and-do-that.

All too often, the Adult World will say, 'They've had enough play, it's time for learning', or the step out of Early Years is seen as a rite of passage, the door closing behind the children as they step into Big School with its desks, grouping and good sitting, good listening and good looking. In this world, the adults separate play and learning, creating the two experiences of the Lesson and Playtime. Play becomes a break from learning. It's as though playtime becomes a rationale for the desk and the table.

And this happens because the Adult World switches off its intrigue. It shuts down its own curiosity. It replaces time with pressure. It fills space with the rush and the push to cram and test and teach, and assembly and interventions and books and rules and sitting and staying in; all the while, children's essential selves are diminishing, all the while being subtly told that they have no space in their own learning. What should have been an adventure, slowly evolves into a mapped-out journey on a treadmill.

At the heart of this is fear because to do anything different we have to open ourselves up to the unknown. This is possibly the one thing that we are afraid of: that if we let go of control, then somehow we can no longer 'see' learning; that if we let go of The Plan, then learning can't and doesn't happen.

Children naturally pursue learning: they are eager for growth. If we are tuned as co-researchers, then we see that children have a busyness, that their self-directed 'activity' is something to understand, that they are more than capable of planning for themselves and that children will actively engage in the pursuit of transformation. It then becomes our role to magnify this rather than control it.

If we don't understand or can't infer a child's learning, then we need to unearth and discover it for ourselves. If we enable children to have more freedom in their school day, then we need to reimagine ourselves in the context of intrigue and curiosity. To do this, we have to make ourselves vulnerable and arguably it's this that is why our schools find 'play' so difficult. Because vulnerability isn't control and because vulnerability isn't orderliness.

And yet, in all truth, it's not about play. It's about something far, far greater that makes the initial vulnerability take on an unsuspected value. It's about magic, and magic is everything.

CHAPTER 11

THE MAGIC OF CHILDREN

'I sang the invitation/I hung on your reply, your verse/Choose me to go into that place with you . . .'

– Place With You, Astronauts, etc.

You've got to love the Adult World when it proudly displays their mottoes or 'mission statements'. Typically, there will be something in there about progress, about community, about academic achievement and happiness.

It's a funny one – happiness. What makes me happy might not make you happy. We could have exactly the same experience but respond to it in very different emotional ways. We can be happy through differing emotions, too. I love horror films – the gorier the better. I am happy watching them, even though at times I have to do this through my fingers or from behind the sofa, or even from a different room. I am happy being scared. You might absolutely hate horror films and never come to the cinema with me.

You might want to go on holiday and sit in the sun on the beach for a week. I would want to go and look at architecture and drink beer in little bars in the shade. Happiness is something that is incredibly difficult to define, and even more difficult to hold on to once we feel it. It's even harder and almost impossible to impose the same experience of happiness on others.

Schools have their mottoes, not for the children but for the Adult World, of course, for the marketplace. There's nothing like the school business manager's selection process of children to choose and how they are going to sit, stand and look in the school brochure. It's an illusion. It's a representation of 'happiness'. And so, the motto feeds the ghost from the past because school shouldn't be about happiness because happiness is easy to fake.

Instead, school should be about **magic**. And the moment we realise that schools should be about magic is the moment that everything has the possibility to change, because it's only then that parents, who have the potential to be the true educational advocates for their children, can start to demand it. And if parents start to demand it, then the fake smiles and the artifice of the school brochure, along with the objectification of children's school experience can be put where it truly belongs, along with the worksheets, the excessive and purposeless homework, the reward charts, the meaning-empty parent meetings and the displays in the entrance of 'best' writing: the past.

So, what is this magic that is just so special? What is the definition that we can share with parents and open up the dialogue with them?

It's all about seeing past the idea that children need to be told a 'single story'. It's about seeing children through a new lens, seeing children as capable of living an index of narratives that we need to explore and discover for ourselves.

Children see the world differently from the Adult World. They have a Seventh Sense: a way of seeing the potential for the world of objects to be something beyond their intended purpose. Through a child's eyes, a box presents the infinite; it offers possibilities for interpretation and reinterpretation. Objects around them exist beyond fixed definitions, each 'thing' shimmering before them with something beyond its 'thingness'. The Seventh Sense is like a hyper-awareness; one might even say that it is like a super power: to see things differently in a swirl of creativity and imagination. For children, the world is something to be interpreted, to be made sense of, to be played with, to be adventured within, to be dreamed.

This Seventh Sense is a gift to the Adult World. In the very moment that we enable children the experiences in which they can use it, we begin to see the world differently, too. We begin to see how the object world is mutable and can be repurposed. In doing so, it begins to impact on our ways of seeing the landscape of our setting, how 'setting up' can place limitations on their ability to 'dream beyond us', how the insistence on challenge cards can negate the potential for children to challenge themselves, how our own sense of fear can quash their desire to take risks, push themselves physically because they want to explore and feel themselves alive within the world.

Each time we see children bring their Seventh Sense to the world, we discover more about them; we learn, we open ourselves to be the learners, the co-adventurers. The more we recognise just how powerful the Seventh Sense can be, the more likely we are to begin the process of control-abdication.

Not only does the Seventh Sense offer you an insight into children and give you a new way of seeing the world, it also gives you an incredible tool to interact with children, too. Some children can have a diminished Seventh Sense. Their early experiences may have eroded their super power. To reignite them, we can use what we know of the Seventh Sense to bring an echo to them once more. We can see how children in the past have reinterpreted the environment and resources; we understand how to think and perceive like a child. We can bring this understanding to our interactions and our co-play so that the child who has less of the Seventh Sense is being empowered *by other children through us*. We become a conduit. **We offer the possibility of the world because children have offered it to us**.

But children offer us so much more than the Seventh Sense. They offer us a magic realm of delight, of wonder and of in-the-moment-livingness. They offer us a reminder of who we once were and how we once were. They offer us a New Future because the things that the future needs are inherently living and breathing inside them, the 'types' of people that the world needs so much is right before us – we just have to look and we have to 'see'.

Often, the Adult World sees children through the Eyes of Grandma. It delights if children can reel off counting to 100; it claps its hands in glee if they can read their reading book; it wants to know from them what they are going to be when they grow up. It's the last bit of that sentence that is children's great undoing. It spins a tale of futurism; it expects children to have a path towards success, unthinkingly confirming to them that what they are right now has less value and that 'success' is quantified by possession and profession.

Children are people right now. They have more attributes than us as adults because they have yet to go through the funnel of the system that channels intelligence, emotion, thinking, imagination, beingness into a narrow definition of curriculum and experience. We emerge from school having 'coped', or having held on to our attributes in spite of school not because of it.

And this is the bitterest of ironies: children have everything the world needs, but by the time they finish their school life, they find that these qualities have on the whole been eroded:

- Creativity
- Curiosity
- Confidence

- Imagination
- Collaborative drive
- Connection
- Communication.

These attributes are a child's 'authentic origin', the driving forces behind their essential self. And it's this essential self which is a child's power and potential. It is the doorway to possibility. It is this that can create a new future, that can uncancel the lost future that we currently offer them. The world needs us to live and bring our authenticity to it – it is therefore critical that we raise this and subsequent generations to retain their authentic origins. Anything less is an erosion of possibility, an erosion of self. Our continued clinging to the past, the Adult World delusional neoliberalism is 'disappearing' children before our very eyes.

In turn, to different degrees, we as adults have been disappeared too. And that's possibly the greatest power that the magic of children can bring to the world: it brings us as adults back to life. When we embrace the magic of children, when we give space and time for children to bring themselves to their learning, then we begin to breathe their ether, see the world through their lens and live once more as creative, curious, adventurous beings, and then we discover the possibility of a resurrection of our own essential selves. Children offer us new life. They offer us adventure, they offer us magic, they offer us the mirror of 'soulification'.

CHAPTER 12

LEAVING THE FACTORY

'Did we lose ourselves again?/Did we take in what's been said?/Did we take the time to be/All the things we said we'd be?'

– *It Means Nothing,* Stereophonics

Several times in the preceding chapters, I've talked about the idea of our children's educational experience needing to be an adventure. It will seem obvious, but they can't have an adventure if they are perennially kept in a factory. Our youngest children can't bring themselves into their learning if they are forever confronted with the spectre of wholeschoolism. There's no magic in a classroom that is dominated by the teacher or by top-down-ology.

The factory school is straight out of the past. Set up for management and monitoring, the day is centred around the production of work-because-we-have-to, with children completing tasks because the teacher gives it to them and an approach that seeks to impose the efficient production on the 'workers'. This model puts the teacher firmly in control, putting ideas in children's heads, transmitting knowledge and information, spoon-feeding and delivering instruction. Success for children comes through memorisation of this information and study for a test. It becomes the environment of the blah-blah and the tick-tock. The school day slowly becomes something to survive and get through. If you don't believe in life after death, then just look at children's faces when they leave school at the end of the day, the sense of awakening joy now that it's over.

Not only is this ghost from the past model of teaching still prevalent, but it's also become even more entrenched. How? Because the concepts of rigour and accountability, the two lynchpins of the neoliberalist agenda which has suffocated so much of our cultural potential and possibility came along and sold the education system the idea that what schools needed was improvement. Private companies swept in with the perfect solution of standardised testing, which could prove the 'failure' of schools and then in turn create the conditions of the market place and profitability – all hail the School Business Manager!

Out of the window went the idea that perhaps children are humans with emotions and background and psyche and dream, and instead in rushed labelling and tracking and spreadsheets and monitoring and failure and rapid progress and interventions and scores and you-can-but-you-over-there-can't, and here's a test and here's another one and, oh, here's another one, and all the time in this great big educational Numberwang comes one thing, sneaking in inside the Trojan Horse of accountability: FEAR.

The factory has no time for personal growth. It has no time for authentic nurture. It has no time for autonomy because there's a test coming. That test is going to define the school. It's going to define the teacher. And here comes the inspecting team and the learning walk and the book scrutiny and the moderation and the observation to make sure you are doing your job properly and in accordance with the system that has been imposed on you as a school and a teacher.

I have heard of an academy chain of primary schools in my own county of Devon that monitors classrooms through CCTV cameras to ensure that teachers across the network are all teaching the same lesson, all teaching what has been prescribed. The blinking red light of the camera, the all-seeing eye, checking, watching. I wonder which blinks faster: the red light or the teacher's heartbeat? In the name of consistency and accountability, fear and mistrust become the watchwords over our educators.

So, through this fear we forget about the most critical cog in the factory: the child. The child just needs to perform. The child just needs to produce. Here's the label, here's the group, here's the work. Because I have to prove. I have to justify. I have to have an outcome and measurability. How are we challenging this group of children? Why hasn't this child made expected progress? Why are these children not performing as well as those children? And with each scrutiny, each week that introduces more and more devel-opmentally inappropriate practice and Adult World unthinkingness, the children themselves begin eroding.

The church of neoliberalism has created the myth of a new Holy Trinity: rigour, accountability and test. In turn, this myth has become a belief, and this belief has become blind faith.

All the while, fear has gripped our education system. The narrative of failure has trickled down to the children and instead of magic, we have created a culture of low self-esteem and disconnection. Everything seems to have become about 'readiness' and anything that cannot be measured as such can just fall by the wayside. The Adult World is suspicious of anything it cannot control or apply its labels to. And that is why play is so under threat and so devalued, because to the Adult World the freedom of thought and expression and creativity doesn't fit easily inside the cells of its spreadsheets.

School is *not* somewhere to survive. School is *not* somewhere that should devalue you. And school is *not* a place where you should have to become disconnected from your essential self just to cope.

The disconnection that the testing agenda has created not only separates children from themselves, from one another, from their teachers and from joy (spend a moment thinking about the irony of schools having a focus on 'reading for pleasure'), but it also disconnects teachers from the children, too. What should be a close bond of nurturing, of support, of adventure is turned into the factory manager pushing the workers to produce and produce more efficiently. The richness of true learning steeped in the generation of ideas, of collaborating as a team, of cooperative engagement, of connection and playing with learning gets boxed up and put away in the attic.

Accountability in turn morphs into blame, the finger pointing to the school, the teachers, to the children themselves, but very rarely does the system point the finger at itself. Instead, here in England, it closes down the early support networks such Sure Start centres and squeezes funding for the sectors that have the potential to stimulate the conditions for connection, more loving parenting, language development, early book love and the spark of hope, but instead of investing in these critical areas, it prefers to absolve the banks and the money-makers with bailouts and tax breaks, or turns its back on tax avoidance and continues the narrative of failure so that private finance can step into the void. And it does this to create the conditions of failure so that the more companies can step in to the education system, the more profit can be made, and all the while children erode, fade and 'disappear', all the while a future with all its unknowns and possibilities is cancelled and the factory remains intact.

And the biggest heartbreak? It's that this model of education is making its way earlier and earlier into young children's lives. It's like a shadow lurking over children with reading schemes being developed for nurseries and handwriting books for three-year-olds with companies attempting to engender fear in parents that their children are somehow deficient and will be left behind by their peers or won't cope with school.

So, it's time for the adventure. It's time to push open the factory gates and leave it behind. It's time to explore alternatives. And if the system cannot change, if it is so determined to disappear our children, then, at the very least, let's give children the longest possible time to have joy and connection. If we really can't see that the spreadsheet is the antithesis of all that education should be, if we have to set our course for profit and measurability, then at least let's explore how we can get the spreadsheet full with its numbers in a different way. Let's investigate how we can give the Adult World what it wants, and all the while continue to be the advocates of childhood.

As Early Years practitioners, it's time to begin the push up, not continue the push down of curriculum and expectations. And perhaps it's about reconfiguring 'Early Years'. Maybe it's the opportunity to show that Early Years practice shouldn't stop at the age 5, 6 or 7, but at 18. Maybe it never ends. Perhaps 'Early Years' *is* 'Education' with no excuses for effective practice to come to an end or at least not to echo with the children as they move through.

Perhaps the phrase 'Early Years' excuses schools to shrug it off or dismiss it, or just give vague attempts to understand it or value it. Maybe it's time for us to demonstrate the power that children have when we enable them and afford them freedom. And yes, this adventure can't be achieved overnight. Yes, it takes little steps to begin with. Yes, it requires courage and faith. Yes, it's a challenge. But something has to change.

So, let's feel the fear, embrace the magic of children and take those first steps into hope, faith and then love.

CHAPTER 13

THE 3MS

'Spinning on that dizzy edge/I kissed her face, I kissed her head/And dreamed of all the different ways/I had to make her glow ...'

– Just Like Heaven, The Cure

The Ancient Greek philosopher, Plato, had an allegory about our perception of reality being a little like a cave with its inhabitants only seeing shadows of real objects on the cave walls, as though they perceive a facsimile of real life and what it is and could be. Some of the cave dwellers slowly make their way out of the cave to discover the world for what it is and all its possibility. They emerge into life and into living – they discover a new lens through which to see the world.

And so, this can be our experience too if we take the step out of the factory with all its machinery and control and constriction of real learning. If we begin to question, if we begin to see that our young children need something different from the diet of restriction and erosion, then we begin to see life once more and the glow of the magic of children.

Heading into the magic of children is an adventure and so needs preparation if we are to maximise our time in it. It's important to note that we are not destroying the factory when we leave it. The factory contains the curriculum alongside the overbearing rules and Adult Worldism. What we are going to do is pack a suitcase of the skills from the curriculum that the Adult World demands and then leave the rest behind.

We are not in a position to overrun the factory or cast out the manager; instead, we are simply going to take the elements that are the objectives we have to achieve with children and put them in the suitcase. The factory owners want output, so let's give it to them, but add to the children not take away from them. We liberate the children in front of us and create the conditions for adventure not adversity, and at the same time we give the Adult World the progress that it demands.

It all comes back to skills. I explored this more fully in *Can I Go and Play Now?*, so what follows is a brief reminder so that we know what it is that we need to take with us on our adventure. It is skills that will create the progress. It is skills that move children forward alongside their natural development, and there are three skills areas that the Adult World is primarily interested in.

This doesn't mean that we are going to value the three more than any other. We are still going to give our children something magic and broad and powerful, and we're going to do this because the 3Ms rely on giving children freedom to bring their creative and collaborative selves to their daily experience. Our environment and our continuous provision will create the conditions for 'soulification' – it's just that we are going to 'report back' on three areas because that is what the Adult World sees. Everything else is hidden from view, but that doesn't mean that we don't value it.

So, the 3Ms are: Making Conversation, Mark Making and Mathematics. Many things in the Adult World rely on making things more complicated than they need to be. However, the simpler we make something, then the clearer it becomes. In effect, we create the verb 'to 3M' and put that in our minds. Then, when we interact with children, when we consider our continuous provision, when we plan any direct teaching on the carpet, one, two or even all three of the 3Ms can be brought out of our mind and into the situation. Anything can be 3Med.

In the next chapter, we'll explore what it is that you base your 3Ming on, but for now it's worth letting it sink in that anything can be 3Med – anything. Counting, measuring, writing, reading, adding, subtracting, grouping, sharing, the list goes on.

You can sprinkle vocabulary – Making Conversation – over any experience. It doesn't need a laminated list in the water zone – you can simply have a canon of vocabulary in your head. Quite simply, think of a word. Let's use the word 'wet'. Now think of or look up as many synonyms as you can so that when you interact with children, you can pull these words out of your head, as if you are taking them out of a library shelf. You effectively extend children's talk by dropping words and modelling sentences into your interactions and because these are in play, they have real context and meaning for them – they become words that they feel able to use with purpose. The added benefit is that because play sees no 'groupings', all children, whether they are confident communicators or emergent talkers, hear the words and sentences together. It's my experience that the confident children then use the words with the less confident ones, something really powerful because children are more open to listening to other children than to adults, and this means that language becomes like a daisy chain from one child to the next.

Listening is a key component to this 3M – it's not all about raining words and sentences down on children. It's why it's called Making Conversation, because it's a two-way exchange, taking turns, showing interest, challenging, questioning, wanting to discover more. Most adults find this hard because most of the time in social situations we find ourselves waiting for a 'chat-gap' so that we can talk about ourselves, our holiday plans, our bills, our marriages, our children, our food shopping, some gossip about Janet down the way or the really 'funny' thing we read online yesterday. Conversation is an art and if we give children the message that it's a one-way barrage of words from the adult, then subtly we signal that their opinions, ideas and observations are of less value than ours. Sometimes it's good to listen and if you find it hard, then place a strip of imaginary masking tape over your mouth or clench your teeth – immerse yourself in child-chat. Of course, if you have children with specific language needs or who are developing the use of words as a second language, you will do more modelling, but be mindful of the potential of the children around you who are might be just as capable of being 'teacher'.

Mark Making is a fabulous world to open up. However, it can be the one area that practitioners find hard to unlock because children aren't developmentally ready to be writers at the age of 4½ – writing becomes something that we have to 'get' children to do, rather than find joy in.

Joy in Mark Making is critical and there is something incredible that we can introduce to children that is really powerful: it's the world of the secret symbol. I've yet to find a child who doesn't love these two things: hiding and finding. Birthday presents, Easter egg hunts, Christmas, sealed boxes, closed doors, parcels, treasure trails, geo-caching, passwords – it's all driven by curiosity, simple cause-and-effect and the element of surprise.

Secrets and discovery are everything for children. In fact, they are everything for adults. I have a secret. A really, really big one. Would you like to know it? Email me and I'll share it with you: greg@canigoandplaynow.com. Some of you may well email me because you want to know, you want to unearth the unknown. In the same way, turn Mark Making into the same experience. Tap into joy, tap into the unknown pleasures of secret symbols.

Secret symbols can be anything, but to begin with they are not letters. Instead, they are circles, lines, crosses, triangles, squares. They can mean anything. Using secret symbols gives children the confidence to make marks because there is no right or wrong. There is no prescribed way of writing them. Yet they carry meaning – a personal meaning and because these symbols can be written anywhere, hidden anywhere, can be interpreted and reinterpreted as children want to use them. They want to hide them: in shoes, under rugs, outside, in trees, in holes, folded inside books, in pockets, under hats. They can go home as symbols for parents, for the family pets, for the shopkeeper on the walk homewards.

Symbols work because they are a message. Writing is a message. We either write a message to ourselves, such as a shopping list, or to others, such as an email or text message. Either way, writing is messaging, which is why I choose to use the word 'messaging' and not 'writing' with young children. Instead of a 'writing table' (are children sparked by those words?) I place a 'message centre' right in the centre of the room and one outside, too. 'To the message centre!' is a really powerful cry for children to hear from an adult. Messaging is something to be excited about because it has purpose, meaning and joy all wrapped into one.

A message centre is a simple arrangement: two tables, six chairs and a bookcase of resources such as different sized and coloured paper, staplers, hole punchers, masking tape, treasury tags, loo rolls, sticky labels, cardboard boxes, string – anything that suggests that it can be used to carry a message. All this alongside some simple sheets of symbols to give children ideas of what they might draw to leave their message. It's not the only place where children can mark make, but it is the place that will be the energy for the learning landscape and when it comes to early Mark Making, energy is everything.

The joy of secret symbols can slowly be morphed into secret letters, secret words, secret phrases, then finally secret sentences: an evolution of symbols and of meaning juxtaposed with the evolution of skills and phonics teaching. And the beauty of secret messages is that you can write on anything. You can leave them around your space for children to find. You are freeing Mark Making from the constraints of a book and instead giving it new life in continuous provision. Very subtly, you are unfolding writing and reading as two intertwining skills that can have meaning for them, that can bring joy, and the moment children discover this for themselves is the moment that the symbolic world of letters and words has the possibility to come alive.

Writing and reading can be about anything, too, because it's about skill, not what something is. It's about emotional connection, children writing about what they want to write about, not 30 sentences about the Hungry Caterpillar all following the same sentence starter. Writing becomes the conveyance of their inner voice, of their delight. It starts to become an act through which their beingness can glow.

And this is the secret, secret message: that children are valued, that adults are not controllers, that the act of messaging is open to all, that meaning can come from children and does not have to be imposed by the Adult World. Through the message centre, writing becomes something I want to do, not what I have to do.

The added bonus to messaging is that messages go home – secret codes, passwords, messages tucked into Velcro on shoes, left for parents to find on the gate. Suddenly, writing starts to go home. Parents begin to show an intrigue, they want to discover this secret. What is happening is that a community is now being reshaped. We now find that adults are showing an interest in what is happening with their children. The teaching of writing has shrugged off a ghost from the past; it has opened up a new possibility. The joy of messages begins to spread outwards.

We have to release writing from its bookishness. The moment writing is in a book it is dead. It is closed up ready to be marked, ready for the highlighter pen. It has no audience. It loses its meaning and its potential. The expectation that early writing belongs in a writing book is the death knell of joy, it is the very coffin of Mark Making.

Underneath the 3Ms are three further secret 3Ms. They are secret because the Adult World is less interested in them because it doesn't necessarily value them as children go through their school life. They are, however, just as important: Muscle and Movement, Mindfulness and Magic.

Muscle and Movement is essential for children. It's really important, therefore, that our provision offers rich potential for climbing, jumping, crawling, throwing, gripping, squeezing, pinching, rotating, pulling, pushing, stretching. Children are not all-day sedentary learners. They need access to physical opportunity in abundance.

Likewise, they also need interactions with educators who are aware of Mindfulness, aware of when to step in with skills or understanding, aware of that fine edge between stealing a moment or magnifying it. There is a fine balance between 'what-I-know' and 'what-you-know' – step in too soon and we run the risk of wrestling control, stand back too often and we risk losing possibilities that are presented. There is an art and, like any art, it is honed and crafted through experience, both successful and less so.

Magic is the final secret 3M, and this is your magic. Your adult magic that you have inside you, which is an echo from your own childhood. It's your ability to see the world through the lens of a child, to see how experiences need to be engaging, motivating and bring joy. If you think like an adult, then you offer something remote. If you reimagine as a child would, then you have a greater chance of forming the bonds that will in turn lead to the co-adventure.

Using 3M with children is what gives them increased freedom. It is not about control. It unshackles us from an over-focus on 'what' children do and instead brings our attention to the skills they demonstrate, to the skills that our provision enables and to the progress that children make once we 3M with confidence.

And we can only 3M if we have faith – faith not just in children, in their capabilities, their curiosity and their ability to choose, but faith in ourselves. It's faith that can transform us. It's faith that changes everything. It's faith that's waiting for you and, once we open our souls to it, then we just need to plan to see the pathways ahead, which is great because the next chapter is going to show you how to do just that.

CHAPTER 14

THE PASSPORT OF PLANNING

'Living day by day isn't everything that it seems/It's just tiny dreams/Man, it's just tiny dreams . . .'

– *Lose Yourself*, The Makeout Club

'The magic of children is a foreign country; they do things differently there' is what L.P. Hartley could have written at the beginning of *The Go-Between*. The way that children see the world, their sense of self and how that functions among the selves around it are all mysteries to be unearthed. Research and understanding of child development can go a long way, but ultimately the key is knowledge of the child who plays before you, and this knowledge is filtered through the lens you yourself look through, how you 'see' children.

Your lens will be reflected by your planning. The more you see that effective, emotionally connecting learning is achieved by loosening the prescriptive grip on planning, the more children have the opportunity to plan for themselves and in turn show you their magic.

Tight planning is the product of control, of a desire to see an explicit structure, a clear path through an academic year. It's what drives the 'death through activity' type of plan: children will do this, then that, then this, and now this and then this. With this type of planning, the Adult World seeks to maintain power and dictate the flow of learning.

A plan based on activity is driven by the past, by the 'niceness' of how provision looks and by the myth that somehow children need to be occupied and directed in order to learn. Yes, it can keep children quiet; yes, it can present a sense of 'viewability' for outsiders, but all the time it is eroding the magic of children by denying them the possibility of interpretation, curiosity, creativity and 'beingness'. The subtle message to children from this type of planning is that learning is controlled by the Adult World and has little room for the soul or authentic connection.

With the 3Ms in our head, however, the lens begins to transform. Now the days become less about 'doingness' and more about 'beingness' and skill. What we are embracing is the idea of 'skill-ability' and in doing so we embrace the magic of children. If we plan for skills, then we are accepting that children are more than capable of planning their own learning, of running with ideas, seeing connections, collaborating and making sense for themselves.

By putting the 3Ms in our heads, we open up the day to take learning anywhere and with anything. We give ourselves the ability to go in any direction because we are not looking for a specific 'doing', but an opportunity to extend or introduce new ideas and skills and challenge thinking. The 3Ms enable us to become the facilitator rather than the instructor. They create the mental landscape inside us to be open-minded, not to 'think straight' but to rethink, reimagine and reperceive.

We begin to have an authentic relationship with children because we are no longer the controller, but instead offer freedom to be active and contemplative. In turn, we become 'conscious educators', aware of children for their 'whoness'. We begin to show them that we have hope and faith and love because we value them. We are no longer disconnected but share a consciousness of one another.

Like the 3Ms, Next Steps Planning is very simple. I explored it in *Can I Go and Play Now?*, so briefly it is one document for each 3M, with a table of progressive skills and then one that summarises the personal attributes that we might find in children – e.g. being socially mindful, confident communicators, having a knowledge of people and the world around them, and being creative. On each document, we move the children's names as they progress through the developmental skills. Planning in this way focuses us on children and enables us to shape our direct teaching inputs, our learning environment, our resources and our interactions so that children are exploring and being 'taught' at the cusp of their understanding and skills set.

In essence, Next Steps Planning enables us to establish what we know about children and then what we don't know, all the while giving us a tool for assessment, observations, play experiences, relationship and ultimately progress. It becomes a document of unfoldingness. We are no longer acting under ticklist-ism. We are enablers and facilitators of growth: we create the conditions so that children can move forward through exploration, relationship and interaction.

The beauty of planning in this way is twofold. It gives the Adult World the progress that it demands while still retaining the essential self of children, but equally it also enables us to interact with children with non-explicit differentiation. For example, several children can be playing alongside us and skills can be sprinkled over the top to each child depending on their Next Step; all the while they are unaware of their 'place', their 'ability', whether they are all the suffocating phrases we have invented for children such as top, bottom, middle, low, high, mastery, developing, emerging, red group, blue group, or Mrs Babbage's reading group – the list goes on and with each utterance of them, we define children, setting their potential in stone.

Next Steps Planning does the opposite – it is based on what we know about children and then their next steps can in effect be infinite: yes, we plan to ensure they are at the cusp of their skills, but they can also experience the next steps of more confident children around them as they collaborate and interact with us. We offer children freedom. We no longer define them or negate the way children learn: they don't 'think straight', they are not necessarily linear in their thought processes but instead exist in a criss-crossology of neurons and connectivity and intrigue. Next Steps Planning is linear to a degree, but it accepts that children can 'think beyond' the Adult World's illusory definitions of self and capability.

Next Steps Planning comes back to the idea of mystery – what have we yet to unearth about the children before us, what are they telling us about themselves and their understanding? Planning is no longer an act of pulling children towards knowledge through the Adult World's pre-planned definitions of experience. Instead, it is a cooperative adventure side-by-side in which both adult and children are immersed in 'not-knowingness', exploring, taking risks, collaborating, democratically enabling one another and discovering skills and capabilities in unison.

Equally important is the question of what they are telling us about our learning landscapes, about our interactions and our parameters: their beingness is under our influence, is taking shape alongside us, it becomes our beingness too. And I think this is a very powerful way to see planning. It's no longer a piece of paper. It's no longer something that controls or regulates experiences. Instead, it becomes a tool for growth, a tool for discovery and a way of ensuring that children are valued for who they are and nurtured for who they are becoming. Because their past becomes their present, becomes their future.

CHAPTER 15

THE GOLDEN TRIANGLE: ENGAGING ENVIRONMENTS, QUALITY TEACHING, EMOTIONAL CONNECTION

'When routine bites hard and ambitions are low/And resentment rides high, but emotions won't grow/And we're changing our ways taking different roads . . .'

– Love Will Tear Us Apart, Joy Division

Our adventure so far has taken us out of the factory, with a suitcase of skills in one hand and a passport of skills-based planning in the other. These three steps are already taking us towards the magic realm of children – we are underway. Key to moving forward is to ensure that we have the Golden Triangle in place. Without it, we will be a stranger in a strange land.

The Golden Triangle is based around the idea of the 'presence of absence' and this emanates from the three corners of the triangle.

Engaging environments

If we are to afford freedoms for children and if we are to create the conditions for them to acquire skills and develop their essential self, then our continuous provision needs to present possibilities not parameters. Central to the notion of freedom is choice. So, our landscape needs to maximise the choices that children can make rather than make them for them.

If we over-emphasise our own version of provision by consistently 'setting up' areas, then we effectively remove choice for children. If we are always theming our zones, then we are sending a subtle message that we retain control over the 'what' and the doingness of the day. Overtly setting up closes down the ability for children to dream, to bring their imaginations to the learning environment.

Our Next Steps Planning is to reflect our understanding that skills are what will create progress, and skills can be applied and developed through any act of doing, not necessarily our closed, prescribed ones. Therefore, the more choice we lend, the more opportunities we offer for children to unfold.

The classic areas of continuous provision can all offer choice – it's just a case of how we present them. The presence of absence in this case is about resisting the temptation to continually have areas pre-ready and set up. Instead, if we offer small baskets of resources for children to choose from, resources that we know will enable the skills, then not only can children bring their imagination to it, they can also rehearse and develop skills either with us alongside or without us. Our interactions become clearer, more precise because we are less controlling over the 'doing' – in fact, by offering provision in this way we also benefit by gaining insight into the 'how' and the 'what' that children are presenting to us. We get to live our intrigue into their world.

One of the biggest mistakes we make in the continuous provision is to cling to the belief that having more of something makes it effective. In fact, it's the opposite. As educators, we tend to be mini magpies, forever on the hunt for resources, bringing things in from home, always wary of throwing things out or passing them on because one day they might just come in useful.

What happens is that unless you have Amazon warehouse-type storage, your space ends up becoming an apocalypse of 'stuffness'. When this happens, it becomes increasingly difficult for children to make a choice. It becomes sensory overload, or we end up with huge boxes of plastic that are then strewn all over the floor like the Great Flood, which then creates stress and temper loss at Tidy Up Time. Children don't need masses of 'stuff' – again, it comes back to simplicity. By making the provision simpler, it becomes more accessible, it becomes more engaging and more open to skills.

Choice also means that each space can be engaging for all children. A lovely space centre for the role play might look great and may attract children initially, but it can't be interpreted easily and may well put some children off entirely, thus minimising the potential reach of that area. It all comes back to the Seventh Sense of children.

The Seventh Sense is children's ability to see through the world of objects and its intended form. They don't see a box as a box. They see its infinite potential to be anything. They don't see a paper plate as a paper plate. They look beyond it and view its possibilities to be something 'outside of itself'. They don't see limitation – they see endlessness.

It's this ability that is at the heart of the mystery of children. It could be argued that it is this that defines childhood somehow. It's what defines the magic realm in which they live and when we ourselves begin to see how they apply it to the world; it is what opens up the potential richness of children's play. The Seventh Sense is the great unknown. It is the mental plan that children have deep within them; it is their thinkingness, their beingness.

The moment children come through the door into our classroom, they bring their Seventh Sense with them. As educators, we don't know in which direction this will take them, but it will be the basis for the adventure if our continuous provision has not drawn the map in its entirety for them. It's why three areas of provision are so critical: woodwork, the creative area and loose parts. None needs to have prescribed outcomes. All can have endless possibility at heart because children will see the choice of resources and bring their Seventh Sense to them in ways that we can never second-guess. And that's because children are infinitely better at planning than we are.

As an aside, the Adult World obsession with 'busyness' is the death knell of the Seventh Sense because the demand for children to be 'challenged' and 'doing' and 'learning' negates the fact that children sometimes need moments of downtime, of boredom, even to reboot, to mull over things, to plan, to process. We tend to over-schedule children, over-structure their experiences so that they are seen to be 'learning' 100 per cent of the time. And the phrase 'seen to be' is an important one because moments of thinking, of piecing together what could happen next and how, are all part of the Seventh Sense, which means the further you remove yourself from children, the harder it becomes to see and see its value.

Quality teaching

This isn't a book about how to teach on the carpet. In a nutshell, don't blah, blah, base any adult-led teaching on skills from your Next Steps Planning; for the children in front of you, be engaging, short and sharp, and if you have to teach pre-planned maths or phonics, do your very best to read the faces of the children on the carpet – they will be telling you everything you need to know.

Emotional connection

Emotional connection is possibly the greatest missing ingredient from our classrooms, our teaching training and our school leadership teams. It's as though 'progress at all costs' is so ingrained in our systems that any sense of wonder, joy or connection to learning gets shelved very quickly or becomes piecemeal. Teachers seem to be brought into the system knowing how to plan, how to monitor, read data and design a lesson. We end up 'doing' topics so that we can deliver teaching, each day presenting children with little to spark them. Some topics do work really well. Some, however, don't. They become things to cope with, to endure. The moment we disconnect children from their day is the moment joy goes out of the window.

Joy comes through the buzz of doing things that excite us. We are all unique and different activities will excite us in different ways. It's why choice is so central. The moment we introduce the idea that children are capable of choosing their learning experiences is the moment we connect them to joy. It's why Next Steps Planning is so powerful because it explores skills, not the doingness. When children actively pursue their own interests, their own Seventh Sense, then joy enters the room.

And it does so because children need freedom and autonomy. They need a positive sense of self to reveal to them how they are as learners, and this can only truly happen if they can choose: zone, resources, playmates, process, outcomes, narrative. When we nullify any of these, then we run the risk of disconnecting children. Similarly, if we always feel that we have to be interacting with children for them to 'learn' and don't find times in the day to observe and discover, then we are in danger of stifling curiosity and possibility – it's a balancing act: adult interactions are essential to enable skills teaching, but equally, the presence of absence can be incredibly empowering for children because it signals to them that we have faith and that we value their time without us in the same way as time with us.

Emotional connection is huge for educators and for children: when we are drawn into play by children and are able to skilfully move learning forward, all the while being drawn into the magic of the Seventh Sense, then this connects us to what unfolds before us. We become co-adventurers, equally as curious and wonderous; we find freedom to interact as co-players and we are invited into the magic.

Children's joy becomes your joy, and it's for that very reason why the magic of children will change your life.

CHAPTER 16

THE MAGIC MIRROR

'But my baby's so vain she is almost a mirror/And the sound of her name sends a nervous shiver/Down my spine . . .'

– *Shivers*, Boys Next Door

We've already explored how children have an 'essential self'. We've already identified that children are capable and curious, creative and collaborative. We can hopefully recognise that children need a sense of autonomy and solidarity within the classroom so that they know they belong and can nurture both themselves and those around them. This is the shape of children. This is their starting point through the Spiral.

Children have a multitude of attributes, a myriad of possibilities within them. The moment we define children through an Adult World lens is the moment that we begin the process of erosion. On an individual level, children need to emerge from our schools with a solid sense of self, with their natural creativity still intact and with their ability to think and act freely without the overwhelming need for instruction.

On a socioeconomic level, children need to emerge with the aforementioned attributes, but also able to collaborate, problem solve, apply 'thinkingness', be respectful and able to engage with debate and challenge and do all these things confidently and in diverse ways. The world of business and entrepreneurship needs adults who are doers, thinkers and feelers, adults who can apply the new to the old, to resolve the mistakes of the past and move the world forward. Ultimately, the world needs 'players'. It needs adults who can toy with ideas, think and unthink, look for solutions, and turn the linear into a labyrinth.

It is why play is a Moral Imperative – it's not a choice. It's not something to sideline because the Adult World decides that it has no value in its systems. Play is critical. This cannot be overstated enough. It is not a choice: it is a fundamental right. If we negate play, with all its wonderful potential, not just at that moment but also in its integral power to shape children into the adults of tomorrow, then we are cancelling the future. If we curtail the chance for children to unfold themselves with us, but instead try to force learning, then each second we do this is a second that has been disappeared in the future.

And herein lies the incredible power of Early Years practice. No longer should it be something to defend. No longer should it be something to protect. When we provide play and creativity and opportunities for self-discovery, no matter how small, we are adding to the possibilities of a New Future. In that very moment of play, we are making a statement, not just about the children in front of us, but all children. We are making a declaration of faith in them, that we have hope through and love for them. We are valuing them, accepting them, recognising their true role: to lead us out of the past and into new possibilities. And to do this, to come out on the front foot and champion play and childhood, we'll need a tool. So, here it is: the Magic Mirror.

The Magic Mirror checks whether we have eroded or added to children. It reflects whether we have given them a 'DIY-store-at-the-weekend' experience. If we have, then the Magic Mirror is telling us something.

If you don't yet have children, then you may not be aware of the 'DIY-store-at-the-weekend' experience. You are possibly in that stage of life where you have nieces and nephews who you love and adore and their company gives you the impression that you will be an insanely good parent and you post photos of yourself with them on Instagram with all the lovely captions of how cute they are and how much they love you. If you believe this is the basis for parenting, then I'm not sure how to break it gently to you: it's nothing like it.

The DIY store at the weekend awaits. The Adult World of tiling, decorating, toilet seats, kitchen appliances, lawnmowers, paint colours, shower curtains, power tools, sheds, lighting, extension leads, bins, taps, door handles and pressure washers stands in the shadows. It's generally not a world for children's emotional connection or positive parenting.

Next time you go to a DIY store, watch the children and look at their faces, observe the disconnection and the parental frustration. The DIY store is not the child's world. It has an Adult World purpose. And it's this that we are trying to avoid in our classrooms. And by classrooms, I don't mean just in Early Years. I mean right through until our children emerge from the education system, either confused, damaged and self-blind or blinking in the bright sun of opportunity and possibility with an intact essential self, ready to truly *be*.

For the Magic Mirror, we need to revisit the idea of what it is children actually are and the richness we need to offer them, and we hold it up to our interactions, our direct teaching and to the continuous provision. Children deserve:

- Choice
- Creativity
- Curiosity
- Collaboration
- Communication
- Core physicality
- Confidence
- Continuing progress
- Commitment
- Connection.

We award ourselves a point for each element that we give to children. If we score more than 7 as a minimum, then we have added to children and the Magic Mirror validates us and tells us to pursue more of the same. Anything less, then we have eroded children and we should either upcycle or, if really low-scoring, possibly consider never doing it again. It's a really simple yet powerful way of looking at ourselves. Have we opened possibilities or have we cancelled them? Have we added or eroded? Given or taken away?

As a process, the Magic Mirror offers us a tool for dialogue, too. It lends us the opportunity to reflect and clarify our vision for children. It enables us to see our own shortcomings as practitioners, our areas for growth. In a way, it acts as a map for us, to make our way through the Spiral, to grow with children and adventure hand in hand.

The real power of the Magic Mirror is that it can be taken upwards through school. It has potential for all year groups to look at the way they interact and 'see' children. It's here that the strength of Early Years education lies. The Magic Mirror sets out a challenge to our leaders, our teachers and our policy makers. If we are happy to accept 3 out of 10, then in essence we are saying that we are happy with the erosion of children. If we are unwilling to offer 7 out of 10 upwards, we are willingly complicit in the 'disappearance' of children and we are guilty of cancelling the future. The Magic Mirror doesn't reflect the soul of children. It reflects the soul of our very self.

CHAPTER 17

A PARALLEL UNIVERSE

'I don't believe in an interventionist God/But I know, darling, that you do/But if I did I would kneel down and ask him/Not to intervene when it came to you/ Not to touch a hair on your head/To leave you as you are/And if He felt He had to direct you/Then direct you into my arms . . .'

— *Into My Arms*, Nick Cave and the Bad Seeds

So, we have our suitcase of skills ready to 3M. We have our passport of planning that will enable us to sprinkle the skills from the suitcase in the right direction and with focus. We have the Golden Triangle that has created the landscape, the direct teaching and the emotional connection that comes when children are afforded freedom to unfold themselves. We are also clutching the Magic Mirror ready to reflect ourselves.

When we have these conditions, when we perceive that play and the Seventh Sense can be embraced in a powerful way, when we can see that children need space, open-ended resources and an authentic relationship with us, it is then that the magic realm reveals itself. It appears like a door made of mini-doors, each one the 'story' of individual children not only in the present but also from the past.

Once this door appears, we just need to choose to step through it. A world of true connection, of wonderment, of the soul awaits. Just step through. And once you do, your task is to keep taking steps forward, further and deeper into the magic of children. It's here that you will find New Life. It's here that we are enabling self-architecture and creating the possibility that the future has the potential for 'otherness'.

It is here that we say a definitive 'yes' to children. And with each step we take, going deeper into the magic of children, if we sing the song of play loudly and clearly, maybe, just maybe, the others who have not yet found the door, who have little or no faith in children, who are blinded by the forces of accountability, might hear the song and something deep within them will respond and want to follow.

You might say that the magic of children is a gift to us. It is something to delight in and be immersed in: to co-adventure with children in a truly transformative experience. Yet, **we** have a gift to give to children. We have a magic realm of our own in which we can co-adventure with them. It's like a parallel universe to theirs. It's a world to explore together, to unfold its secret. It has richness and hope and faith and love within it, layers of landscape to unearth. This place is the world of Story. And the key to unlocking the door to it isn't play – it's a little thing called Drawing Club.

'Oh, my goodness, he just said that the key isn't play! He spent all this time talking about play and how powerful it is and yet here he is saying that there's some Not-Play. What's happening here? Am I dreaming? Is this a nightmare?'

You read it right. Drawing Club is Not-Play. And it's Not-Play for one very simple reason. We want to open the world of Story to children, but we don't want it to dominate the continuous provision, negate the Seventh Sense or erode their self-architecture through exploration of open-endedness. We'll introduce the world of Story through sharing the wonder of Story with all children and utilising it to teach an array of skills in a short session of Not-Play.

We keep Story as a parallel universe that has the potential to step across – it isn't about subjugation and control of the space or of play interactions per se. We have set up a landscape for children to bring themselves into, we have planned our interactions and resources so that skills are at the very forefront rather than 'doingness' and we are going to be spending a large proportion of our time co-adventuring in their world – Drawing Club is a portal into the world of Story that we will open for a short time. It's like making gravy in a jug where you have the little bits of gravy powder that won't ever seem to mix in – Drawing Club is like one of those – a nugget of skills, a mini-adventure that is mixed but isn't mixed at the same time.

We open the world of Story because if we value its enormous potential, then we will want to embrace all the possibilities it presents. Drawing Club is not about control. It's not about 'adult-knows-bestism'. We are unlocking two worlds to explore: Play and Story. Both are highly valuable. Both are shared, but the world of Story is one that needs to be brought to children because it lies outside of their immediate 'Play Consciousness' – we take their hand for that moment and immerse them in something magical, allowing skills from each world to cross-pollinate and add to the richness of the other.

Both worlds require the Adult World to 'see' children for who they are, and both are rooted in narrative, in language and in the expansive galaxy of imagination. Both worlds contain mystery, both offer adventure and the ability to bring about change. Both worlds when you enter them, are like meeting someone who shows you something about yourself or the world that tips you upside down because they reveal a new part of life, of being-ness. They unlock a new part of your 'story' and add a richness that only magic can truly bring.

In essence, both worlds have the notion of 'story' at their heart. Children are telling you the story of their essential self when there is co-adventure in play. Similarly, when we are telling and sharing stories with them, we bring tales and wonder from the distant past, open their minds to the intimacy of the reader/author/illustrator experience and create the conditions for them to explore the dreamtime of story with all its potential for imagination and declaration of the self. We dream wider, we dream deeper, we dream longer and we dream together.

PART 2

DRAWING CLUB

CHAPTER 18

CLUBS

'I wish that I could be like the cool kids/'Cause all the cool kids, they seem to fit in . . . '

– *Cool Kids,* Echosmith

I live in a hilltop hamlet in Devon, England, a scattering of houses backed by a giant wood with views for miles and miles across Dartmoor. To live here possibly requires a certain character since the nearest shop is a drive away and there's no pub. We do, however, have a disused red telephone box, lots of dogs, a fair few feral children and a not inconsiderable amount of eccentricity. Living in the middle of nowhere means that the importance of community is more magnified, so it often leads to a large degree of chattiness, and one such person, who is very chatty indeed, is Pippa.

She'll kill me if she reads this and I've 'over-aged' her, so I'm not going to say in writing how old I think she is, but let's just say that she's retired. It was a conversation with her that brought about the genesis of Drawing Club. 'Never retire early,' said Pippa. 'If you retire early, then you have to leave the energy of younger people that you work with and then spend most of your time with people your own age and nobody wants to do that. You start having to go to lots of clubs to be around younger people, but it's not the same. Stay in work for as long as you can – it keeps you young. There's no club quite like the club of work.'

The idea of belonging, of welcome, of solidarity is incredibly powerful on a human level. It goes back to the concept of Inspiration, Vitality and Acceptance – the requirements for the soul to flourish. Clubs can be instrumental in giving us these. They also feed a desire to be part of something outside ourselves. To an extent, clubs 'normalise' us. They say, 'You like this. We like it too, let's like it together.'

Clubs also have the ability to make activity glow with magic even though potentially they don't. Chess Club anyone? Now, I love a game of chess, but I wouldn't sacrifice too much time playing it. There's a club? You can play chess there? With other people who play chess? Where do I sign up? The word 'club' presents a level of 'coolness' – it validates. If I wanted my son, when he was younger, to do chores at home such as tidy up, stack the dishwasher or weed the vegetable patch, then clubs came to the forefront. There's a club? It's Dishwasher Club? You've never seen a dishwasher being emptied with such vigour. Weeding Club? You get to pull weeds out of the soil? And it's a club, you say? The weeds didn't stand a chance.

Being in a club gives us instant emotional connection. It tells us that we belong and that we are special. We are having a shared experience that is meaningful and that we can contribute to. A club is solidarity and it has membership – it offers a sense of exclusivity and the opportunity to collaborate and develop. So, it's the perfect phrase to use when it comes to education. We offer after-school clubs, breakfast clubs, Forest School clubs, but then compress experience in our schools into 'lessons'. If we rebrand elements of the day into the concept of a club, then we maximise the potential for children to connect with it. We lift it from the humdrum of schooling and add an air of something special.

If you have to do 'guided reading' in your school day, can you think of anything less exciting than telling children that it's time for guided reading? If you are a typical child, is your heart going to respond positively to those words? I would argue 'no'. We have to think like children. We have to put ourselves into their shoes. The experience might not be the most exciting in the world but if, through the language we use, we can at least create the conditions of anticipation, then the children's engagement has a greater potential for focus and 'learning'.

If you are a child, would you like to go to guided reading or would you prefer to go to Cosy Club? Both are the same thing and I'll tell you the answer: it's Cosy Club. I know this because I've run parallel guided reading groups with the two alternate names and the children in Cosy Club engaged more attentively and over time read with more confidence and interest than the children in 'guided reading'. The very phrase 'guided reading' means very little to children. Cosy Club, on the other hand, has a wealth of possibility:

it suggests that the experience has warmth and connection. It also happens to be the name of a chain of bars in the UK, but the children don't need to know that!

Emotional connection is key to the Drawing Club. We want the children to come because we have a world to unveil with them. We want them to bring themselves to it, because in Drawing Club, children are going to come to you. It's here that you need to decide for yourself what that means for you. We'll explore the how and what in subsequent chapters, but at this point we're going to need to decide 'when'. Drawing Club is best done at a table. Drawing Club is going to bring children to you. It is going to bring them from their magic realm into ours – it's how we minimise the impact of this that counts.

I strongly recommend that you run a Drawing Club pretty much first thing in the day and that you do it five days a week. It follows a short input and then children will be going into the continuous provision. So, it means that at some point they are going to leave it to come to Drawing Club. If you make it engaging, then they will want to come. In fact, children often go off and create their own Drawing Club.

When it's time to come to Drawing Club, children come with a huge amount of anticipation because they are now 'in' the club and they have something to 'say'; they have a story to share together. And, if you do it every day, you'll discover that it's the only time you need to call children to you and will free up increased time for you to go into their magic realm afterwards. It gives them access into the world of Story and then access into the world of Play.

It also hugely validates children's play without an adult. We are subtly telling them that they don't need us all the time and that they can explore without us – the presence of absence. Pick your moment to bring them to the Drawing Club. If a child is deeply engrossed, then consider waiting – Drawing Club is not 'grouped', so we are not 'looking' for a set of children. It will be down to your judgment in that moment – the world of Story awaits; it's just finding the perfect time to open it.

CHAPTER 19

THE GREAT BIG BEAUTY OF STORY

Green green youth/What about the sweetness we knew?/What about what's good, what's true/From those days?'

– Carry Me Ohio, Sun Kil Moon

It was my mum who opened up the world of Story to me. Earlier, we explored the happy memories from childhood and primarily these were outdoors, playing with friends, lost to time. Yet, there was another experience in which time just seemed to slip away. It was when I sat on my mum's lap or squidged in next to her to hear her read a story book – tales of shipwrecked pirates and talking horses and monsters under the bed and shopping trips gone wrong and animals going on picnics and the sun always shining while boats glided down endless rivers caressed by the fingers of dozing willow trees.

The magic that poured from those pages. The places we went to and the dreams that it stirred within me. The way that the characters seemed to follow me out into the world of Play, feeding my imagination and creating layers of infinite possibility. It was as though a library of words and emotions and joy was being built within me, adding to the piece-by-piece architecture inside. What a gift she gave me. What pleasure to feel the warmth of a parent so close to you, the lullaby voice and the gentle touch of hand or even the sensation of her thin, woollen M&S cardigan against my face as I snuggled into this shared adventure that we went on, all the while sat on the flowery sofa in our East Midlands housing estate, like some Great Escape.

That was in 1976. Fast forward to now and it would seem as though, along with outdoor adventurous play, the art of 'book-snuggling' is diminishing. Time for family is condensed and restricted. Parents live in a world of pressure and no time. There always seems to be something outside of us, which means that time to just stop and be is ever limited.

The outside world is of endless housing in place of the open spaces that were once the rich landscape of imagination and freedom; the roads on which we invented a myriad of games are now increasingly choked by traffic; the world seems restricted and unsafe, with more and more time spent inside in front of TV and screen. Sharing a book requires time and it's time that neoliberalism robbed us of. It replaced the solidarity of family with the allure of objects and enslaved us to profit and accountability.

Drawing Club, however, gives us the perfect opportunity to replicate 'book-snuggle'. It represents a door for children to step through into a new kingdom and discover for themselves the joy of sharing stories. If it is a dying art, then let's revitalise it, let's build libraries of worlds inside them too so that we maximise the opportunity for story to survive and thrive. In a way, we are acting like portals into the past, bringing voices from long ago into the present, echoing them so that they might live into the future.

There is possibly no greater joy than revealing the world of Story to a child, with all its otherness, all its unpredictability, its strangeness and its beauty. To see the look of surprise or delight on their face, to know that the characters will follow them out from the pages of the book, that they realise that Story is a special friend who can live inside them is one of the most amazing experiences.

Equally, children can live inside stories, too. They can enter the world of imagination to discover strength, to envisage themselves in a character's shoes, to gain empathy, to learn how to handle bigger emotions and to see that there is a hidden solidarity in stories: what we might be feeling in that moment has been felt before; it has been met before and will be met again.

Stories give children a safe space to adventure and to question. The more we share stories with children, the more they begin to see that the worlds within them are as real as ours, are as 'felt' as ours. There is malevolence, mystery, mortality and magic. There is threat and fear and overcoming and belief and goodness and risk and endurance and optimism and promise in the same way that there is in the adventure through the Spiral. It's as though there is a Story Spiral, too, interconnecting and echoing, and when children see that this Story Spiral is in itself a co-advenuturer, then maybe, just maybe, it is the moment that they perceive books as a friend and not an enemy.

One of my favourite words is 'kooky'. Stories are kooky because they are out of the ordinary. They offer us a world of otherness. It's a world that we innately want – we want kookiness in life, we want there to be 'more-than-there-just-is'. We don't question stories when a sheep asks to go for a boat ride, or a monster eats a boy, or a duck drives a truck, or a boy called Max sails away for a year and a day. We want it to be so.

We accept it because we hope for it. We hope that there is something out of the ordinary in life, and the more we hear that this is the case, then our hope turns into faith because we expect it and believe in it. And then, as we've explored with the magic of children, faith turns into love, and don't we want children to love books and stories, to co-adventure with a sense that something magical might just happen and the pages of a book or the words that spill from us as we spin a tale are for falling in love with?

When we adventure with the children before us, we can open doors to new cultures, to the past; we can present new conundrums to solve; we can play with words; we can surprise; we can shock, and we can calm. Stories can take children anywhere in the same way they once did to a little boy with blond hair and a red home-knit jumper sat snuggled with his mum on that flowery sofa in a 1970s East Midlands housing estate.

CHAPTER 20

THE GREAT BIG BEAUTY OF DRAWING

'I have a picture pinned to my wall/An image of you and of me and we're laughing and loving it all . . .'

– Hold Me Now, Thompson Twins

When I trained to be a teacher, my very first placement was in a primary school that was on its knees. The children were hugely disconnected, as were the parents. There was little or no respect for teachers and what teaching went on was half-hearted and seemed more about getting through the day than skilling or engaging the children. In my particular Year 3 classroom, the blinds on the windows were permanently down because the teacher didn't like the sunlight and so it felt like being in a room of lab rats under harsh strip-lighting. Lessons such as P.E. were nearly impossible because the teacher had really tight rules about how she wanted the sessions to happen, but this was at odds with the pent-up energy from the children who had spent all of the day sitting in a chair.

In my heart, I knew that if I was going to survive the placement, I would have to do some thinking. First, up came the blinds, off went the strip-lighting.

I took parts of maths teaching outside. I opened up the door so that fresh air came in. I made my lessons as physical as I could and broke them down into smaller chunks so that I was reflecting the children not a timetable. In P.E., I asked the children what equipment they'd like to explore and then democratically decided on how we could use it safely and respectfully. Within three weeks, the culture within the classroom had shifted. Children seemed to want to be there. Parents were more intrigued about what their children were doing in school. I made mistakes along the way and I got things wrong, too, but in that six-week placement I was determined to give children something different and more from the heart. It wasn't perfect; it wasn't always easy, and I certainly learned lots of lessons. And one of those lessons was the power of drawing.

In that classroom there was a little girl called Tallulah. She was a lot smaller than her peers and she really struggled with school life – her speech was quite poor, and she found herself quite isolated at times. However, during the placement she began to transform. She began to show increased confidence and engage more in learning – she began to glow.

At the end of my placement, as I was dismissing the class for the final time, Tallulah handed me a small folded piece of paper and ran out to her mum. Later that evening I unfolded it and there was a drawing of me and her with a simple sentence: 'thank you for being my teacher'. I still have that piece of paper in my wallet. I haven't kept it because of the sentence. I have kept it because in the drawing, she and I are holding hands and she's smiling. It's a reminder of why I am so passionate about children and trying to bring change for them. It's a reminder of the great responsibility that I shoulder as an educator. It's also an echo from the very day that I learned that drawing is extraordinarily powerful.

When children draw, something very magical takes place: they are creating a representation of the outer world but through the lens of their inner world. In the act of drawing, imagination becomes 'real'. With each line, a metamorphosis takes place, a mental imagery comes to life before our very eyes. What was empty becomes non-empty. What had hidden meaning reveals itself.

Drawing constructs meaning both for the child and the world around them. It is a message – 'Here I am. This is me. This is how I perceive my beingness and my being-in-other-ness.' It is language beyond language – children speak through drawing and do so beyond culture or oral communication. They bring their 'story' to life through creation, through the lines and shades as they take shape.

It is light years away from just being 'a nice thing to do' or a holding activity. And it isn't colouring in. When we offer this, we are subtly sending the message that the child is not enough; we frame their creativity within our own. True drawing is the form and its content, and comes from the child and can never be prescribed to colour in because creativity is their imagination, not our stunted form of it.

And when we combine drawing with Story, it is extra magical because we see how a child's imagination perceives our Story World. When we open up all the richness of Story to them, when we create the conditions for interpretation and reinterpretation, then we construct a bridge between the world of the magic of children and the world of Story.

In the same way that there is no 'right' in secret symbols, there is no 'right' in drawing. There is no 'being good'. If we ask adults if they are 'good at drawing', then the vast majority will say 'no'. They do this because they have been programmed into self-deception. Their time in schools has taught them that outcome is all, that somehow art and creativity is something to be judged. It turns creativity into competition: who is the best? who has value? – all these subtle or not so subtle messages chipping away at children's sense of self.

Drawing Club is the antithesis of this experience. It values drawing. It teaches skills but does not overly critique them. It makes the process collaborative not insular – when we have faith that children will support and assist one another when they draw, we are amazed at their solidarity and respect.

And the real joys of Drawing Club?

- Language acquisition and contextual use flourishes.
- Physical development accelerates.
- Authentic relationships with children grow.
- Progress in reading, writing and maths, the very thing your school craves, goes whoosh.

And the real joy of joys?

You are soulifying children, because not only does Drawing Club open up the world of Story with all its richness, mystery and potential, but at the same time it enables the world of children's magic to exist in school and, if you pair it with Play Projects, you have the possibility of continuing the adventure that is soulification when, for the final time, the doors of Early Years shut behind the children because it can follow with them.

CHAPTER 21

LANGUAGE

'Come a little bit closer/Hear what I have to say/Just like children sleeping/We could dream this night away . . .'

– Harvest Moon, Neil Young

I love spending time with children, but there's other company that I love even more: it's time spent with dogs. Dogs came into my life at a relatively late stage, but they changed everything. There is nothing better than a long walk in the woods in the company of two little dogs called Bonnie and Eppie. Dogs love you unconditionally. No matter what, they want to know you. They 'see' you without judgement or discrimination. If only they could talk with us. Maybe it's better that they can't. Maybe that's what makes them such great companions – they are content in silence with us.

Perhaps communication is both a blessing and a curse? Language elevates us, yet has the potential to destroy us. It can convey the purest emotion, yet can crush us into the ground and divide communities with hate and mistrust. It is arguably the most powerful tool and equally the most power-ful weapon. But it also seems to be a dwindling one. Language acquisition

within our youngest children is less strong. Children coming into our settings have less command of the basics of communication. The reasons
being put forward are many, but centre around the realities of family life
and its pressures on time together, the dying art of 'book snuggling', the
explosion of electronic devices and the erosion of formative positive play
experiences.

Like drawing, language is what brings us into the world. It is how we
share what is inside of us with what is outside of us. It is the expression of
self, of our internal world, the world of imagination and dream. It is our
connection to otherness, our route to solidarity. The collaborative nature of
play with all its exchange of ideas and wonder relies on children being able
to listen, respond and construct meaning together. It brings us 'out of our
selves' and is the key to initiating and extending play with others. Which is
why Drawing Club, when it introduces language, focuses on words that can
be 'played with'. Lots of approaches to language development are literacy
based – e.g. you can't be a good writer if you're not a good talker. If we
value play and children's thinking within it, however, then we should perhaps focus on giving a gift that they can use in the more meaningful
contexts of their play interactions.

Drawing Club exposes children to the world of synonyms by using Story
as a platform. Each week, six to eight new words are introduced as the first
part of the input, each word with its own action to create a physical experience and one in which children can create their own group ones
democratically. These words are based around the story but presented as
being both part of the story but equally part of play. We want children to
see that words are not just for when they are writing to please the teacher.
Instead, we want them to see themselves as powerful communicators and
able to use language for their own purposes – we create a diverse lexicon
within each one of them.

Teaching words in this way does several things. It exposes children to
hundreds of new words across the year and by showing them that these
words can be used when they are playing collaboratively, we create the
potential for children to teach these words to one another, to share their
use of them and to collaborate in language too.

When children begin to use the language that we have shared with them,
several things happen. Because we are presenting language as 'choice' –
e.g. we can choose the words we say – children begin to reflect more on
the words they use with one another. We start revealing that the words have
a power and that how we use them has consequences – it's the beginning
of becoming a conscious communicator, developing an awareness of the
listener and that what we choose to say has an effect on them. We open
the door to the idea that language has a morality and, at the same time,
because it is a key component in it, so does play. If we want positive experiences between us, then the words we choose have an important role in
shaping that positivity.

Possibly even bigger is the delight and joy that sharing language has on young children. It feels good to develop the words you say, to use them in the appropriate context, to teach them to others and to discover that words can be played with as much as building blocks or Lego.

Words can be funny. They can be twisted and mispronounced for effect. They can be joked around with and be the source of invention. Words can be creativity. They can enable us to role-play without being in the role-play area. They can be used to tell stories even though we're not anywhere near the 'book corner' or the 'learning mat'. If we want to be outside and experiment with our voices and how we say words, then we can. We are giving children the freedom to play with language. It isn't fixed. It isn't learning words so I can be a better writer. Instead, I learn words so that I can learn about and become even more of myself *first and foremost*.

We can play with words, explore them and indeed, go on an adventure with them. Children love making up new words for things, they love creating their own 'language', their own label system for the world around them. We are not trying to control language: we are trying to set it free. When we do this, we are adding another layer of intrigue and mystery to our children. We are inviting them to become even more complex, more enigmatic. In doing so, we are expanding the world of children's magic, giving us even more landscape to co-adventure in.

CHAPTER 22

STORY TELLING, BOOKS, TIME OUT OF JOINT

'I feel this place/I'm wide awake/More than ever . . . '

– I Feel This Place, Goldensuns

Drawing Club is based around a repeating cycle of story:

Week 1: story telling.

Week 2: story book.

Week 3: time out of joint.

So let's take a look . . .

Do you have a basket of books by your chair that you read with your children at home time? How did those particular books find their way into the basket? If you put them in there, what was the 'why' behind it? Are they personal favourites? Are they just nice? Do they have tons of words in them? Are they in there just so you have something to read at hand?

If we are going to open up the world of Story to children, let's at least make it the best of all possible worlds. Let's maximise the magic that lies within it. If we don't, then the message to children is that this world is not worth bothering with. We need to emotionally connect them to the world of Story, and books about animals having a picnic don't necessarily connect children hugely. If children are going to come on an adventure with us, then let's make it an exciting one. There is lots of Adult World desperation about boys' achievements, so if we are going to enable boys (and girls for that matter), we need to give them stories that will reach out of the pages to them. And one way of doing this is to scare them.

To a degree, all children get a buzz out of being scared. Obviously, there are levels of fear that we need to be sensitive to, but the principle is that we want to grip the children into our world of Story for five sessions of Drawing Club. A dull book will lead to the Switch Off, whereas we want the Switch On. We want fascination and intrigue and doubt and a sense that at any moment something might go wrong, but an answer lies ahead if we press on with the adventure. The stories we choose need to add to the soulification of children, not diminish it.

We are looking for stories that are going to get the children 'going'. Characters such as witches, skeletons, dragons, wizards, ghosts, zombies, wolves, foxes, monsters, trolls – any mild malevolence we can get our hands on. We reach into the past and bring forth traditional tales that tap into the fears of our collective unconscious, those tales that warn us, that suggest that the world can go wrong and there might just be a chance that for some characters it never comes right again. Threat is everything because that is the signpost towards the magic. If a story just happens, dum-de-dum-dum-de-dum, then deep down no one particularly cares. We want children to open themselves to the world, to feel and imagine and reimagine.

When we immerse ourselves into oral storytelling, bringing these traditional stories to life, with wonder and character voices and our own joy, then the room will be gripped – we want edge-of-the-seat storytelling as though anything might and probably will go wrong at any moment. This is the tradition of storytelling – when you engage in it, you are engaging in history. You are not only reaching back into time for stories, you are reaching back to bring the past itself into the present. You are continuing richness and being empowered by it.

It's the same principle when it comes to story books. We need surprise and threat. Pop-up books, lift the flap, slow turning of pages and wondering out loud. We need Bernard being eaten by a monster, witches in kitchens and strange beasts coming upstairs for their hairy toe.

So many times we lose impetus with stories because we get bogged down with 'book talk', as though children care that 'This is the title' or 'This is so-and-so, she's the illustrator. An illustrator is the person who draws the pictures . . . ', and the clock hand tick-tock, tick-tocking and the children slowly losing the will to live in the world of Story. With books, we need to get pace and get in there – we need joy and delight because if we don't have it and show it, then neither will the children.

The books we choose for Drawing Club need to be short. Long books are best used at the end of the day perhaps as a shared, sustained 'snuggle-in' with children. If a book takes longer than five minutes to read, then I'd suggest it is too long for Drawing Club. I've found that a brief moment of wonder before opening the book adds the necessary hook – 'You're not going to believe what happens in this book . . . ', 'You'll never guess how one of the characters gets away from the baddie . . . ', 'I wonder if any of you have ever met a fiercesome monster on the way home from school? The characters in this book did . . . '. Using phrases like these adds to the mood that we want to create: let's call it PMT – Pre-Magic Tension.

In the same way that storytelling gives way to story books, story books then give way to Time Out of Joint. This is the week that you go back to a different type of storytelling – children's cartoons from the 1970s and 1980s. They don't make them like they use to – believe me. There's something other-worldly for children when they watch *Wacky Races* or *Jamie and the Magic Torch* or *Mr Benn* or *SuperTed*. It's as though you have stepped out of the Tardis bringing a treasure trove of delight with you, from the theme tunes that are all brass band pizzazz to the canned laughter, from the slightly out-of-sync animation to the over-dubbed voices. The children won't know what's hit them.

If you grew up in the UK in the 1970s and 80s, then something else happens as you show them to your children – you become emotionally connected because you are revealing something that was important to you, that is part of you, which as an educator can emotionally be very powerful. And if you didn't grow up with them, or just know of these shows through hearsay, then you are in for as much a treat as the children – you'll unearth something special together, which in a way makes the experience even more of the perfect kind of co-adventure.

CHAPTER 23

MODELLING

'Wind in the wires and you don't know where it's coming from/Be my, be my, be my silver star . . . '

– *In Your Bright Ray*, Grant McLennan

When you have a face for radio, it's a struggle to think what one might model if the chance arose. I'd probably be best off as a shoe model. Either way, when it comes to Drawing Club, modelling is key.

Whether we are sharing an oral story, a story book or Time Out of Joint, we will be focusing on it for just one week. Now, of course, if your children are loving the story and you think that there is more to explore, then hopefully, you'd have faith in yourself to continue. However, one week is ample to adventure with because we don't want it to grow stale – the moment that happens, then we are closing the door to the magic world of Story.

Having shared the 'text', we are then going to model draw on the board to all the children. Loosely, the week looks like this:

Monday: character.

Tuesday: setting.

Wednesday to Friday: adventure.

This is the point at which the fact that school eroded your sense of innate creative power is actually a positive thing. We are going to model draw, so the last thing children need to see are Michelangelo-esque sketches. We need to draw simply. We are not trying to mimic the illustrations from a story book either. We are creating our own version.

So, on Monday we model draw our favourite character from the story. It's more gripping if we draw the 'threat' character. However, when it's the children's turn to draw, they can choose whichever character they like. And it's now that we can sprinkle even more language over the top of what we do. As we draw, we talk about what we're drawing. If it's a monster, then we use words like 'straggly hair', 'beady eyes', 'razor-sharp teeth' – we draw attention to the features of the character because not only does that enable children to access your thinking, it also adds additional words to their lexicon. If you throw in four or five new phrases or words each day, then that could be an extra one thousand words or so that children are going to hear each year.

On Tuesday, we wonder about the setting and again simply draw it, drawing attention to the details that we add, sprinkling vocabulary as we do so.

On Wednesday to Friday, we are going on an adventure with the story. We do this because that is what Story is – it's an adventure and an adventure can happen anywhere. If we stick with a weekly model that repeats the same thing each day, children very quickly lose connection because they are no longer leading but are following you. Going on an adventure places the children right at the heart of the experience. So, for three days we wonder about the story, we invent and we reimagine.

Let's take *Not Now, Bernard* as an example. On Monday we draw the monster. On Tuesday we draw Bernard's house. On Wednesday we wonder what Bernard tasted like and draw things to take the taste away. On Thursday we wonder what vehicle his Mum and Dad might use to escape the monster who is now in Bernard's bed and then on Friday perhaps we consider sending in an even bigger monster from the Rent-a-Monster Agency to get the monster out of the house.

The kookier you make your wonderings, the more children will connect with the world of Story. Anything can happen in a story, so let it. The more you think about where a story might go, the more you connect to it, too, because you invest in bringing it to life. Character and setting are constants because we want children to see that stories revolve around 'doing' and 'being' – they are equally characters in their own setting and correlating them is yet another way to bring the worlds of Play and Story together. And just as in Story, Play can go anywhere. Play can be whatever we wonder – we are providing a constant of 'doing' and 'being', but then unfolding a landscape in both worlds in which to adventure.

Growing up, there used to be a children's annual called *Look and Learn*. It was wonderful because the illustrations had so much energy that seemed to pour out of the pages. In a similar way, Ladybird books possessed the same magic – I used to sit for hours with them, not reading, but instead getting lost in the pictures, micro-worlds of farms and sunny beaches and foxes running through hay fields and swallows gliding effortlessly through blue skies dotted by pillow clouds and in the distance, rolling hills with a scattering of tiny houses. The detail was everything.

And it's the detail in our drawings that is going to be powerful too. It's not about artistry, it's not about being 'good'. We are simply noticing details. In a way we are teaching children to 'look and learn'. Earrings, necks, buttons, shoelaces, hairbands, collars, stripes, polka dots, ears, eyebrows, eyelashes, rosy cheeks, freckles, hair across one eye, pupils, nostrils, Velcro straps, necklaces, boots with heels, zips, window frames, smoke from chimneys, flower petals, apples on trees, the lines that show a character or vehicle is moving quickly, fingers, fingernails, rings, tattoos, pockets, beards . . .

Not all at once, by the way! We are going to drop these in as we progress our drawings, each new drawing presenting opportunities to notice detail. And if you choose to draw maps for characters to find their way home when you adventure out the story, then these present the perfect way to introduce shark fins, rippling rivers, snow-capped mountains, reeds in quicksand, dark caves, pirate ships, skull and cross bones, zombies . . .

We aren't overtly expecting children to include these details in their drawings – they are a possibility that we are presenting to them. When they draw, we wonder 'what else we might add?' or, if they draw a character with no feet, we wonder 'how they might wear shoes if they go to the shoe shop?' – we wonder out loud. Brilliantly, however, so do the children. They begin to see the solidarity of drawing, that it can be a collaborative experience, that they can 'look and learn' from one another, each child seeing something new or different from the next.

The drawing we model is left on the board. We leave it there if there are children who want to use it as a basis for their own drawing. It's a potential scaffold, nothing more. Children don't copy it perfectly – we are not showing children 'the way' to draw, we are showing them 'a way'. They are not replicating your drawing. We have to recognise that some children will want to use your picture because they may lack confidence initially – this phase doesn't seem to last long and it isn't 'wrong'. We sensitively encourage these children to explore new ways of representing their imagination – we lend them ours to spark their own.

'All lovely,' I hear you say. 'But so what? I work in a school. My school wants outcome. Drawing is great but I have the Adult World to consider . . . '

Relax. There's a key ingredient I've not told you about. It's the 3Ms again. You're going to 3M Drawing Cub. And when you do, you will be blown away by it.

CHAPTER 24

THE 3MS AND THE CONNECTION TO DRAWING

'I'm always looking for signs/Looking to read between the lines . . .'

– Looking for Signs, Leif Erikson

We are actually 3Ming when we are sprinkling vocabulary while we are model drawing. We are 'Making Conversation', adding to the language library of all the children within the context of revealing our imagination. As something takes shape before the children's eyes, we are commentating on what is being revealed.

When our drawing is complete, it's then time to add the extra 3Ms. This is the moment that we need purpose. What we are about to write needs to have meaning. It's where secret symbols going right the way through secret letters, then phrases, then finally to secret sentences come into their own. We are writing them because if we don't, then something will or won't happen. Some mild malevolence will take place. The character will lose their way, they will fall off a cliff, the door won't open, a misdemeanour will befall them, the car won't start, something will land on them, their bottom will fall off, they will be sick, they will be invaded by zombies. It's not about writing something dull like 'The monster is in the garden'. Nobody cares. Dig into your imagination and search for your malevolent side.

When the children draw, they will or won't want something bad to 'happen', so they will be connected to a purpose – they want to change the potential, they want to reimagine.

It's here that you need your passport of planning, your next steps. Child A might be working on pencil grip, so will be exploring secret symbols. Child B might be more confident and might be writing a CVC word. Child C might be super confident and ready for sentence writing. All three, however, will be averting disaster, will be telling a story, will be working at the cusp of themselves. And the beauty is that because the children who sat with you in Drawing Club are disparate, they are a random group, a labyrinth of ability, of imagination, of confidence. Just because a child isn't confident with a holding a pencil doesn't mean that they don't have a great imagination and vice versa. When we bring children together in solidarity, then they lend each other their skills – they talk, they wonder, they help one another, they challenge each other. A group of six children become a team. They collaborate with one another – drawing becomes a collective experience.

So when children come to Drawing Club there is a myriad of adventures to go on. You can explore Mark Making through symbols and all the progression to secret sentences. You can do the reverse and write messages for children to read on the back of their drawings. Again, these messages will be at the cusp of their phonic knowledge because you are writing it for them only. We tell them that the secret message is keeping the bad characters away from us, or that if we read it, the character will come and eat the teachers, or that if we read it, something good will happen like burgers and chips will appear for the character – you will know the children with you. You will know what grips them. We are spinning a story with them in that moment. We are presenting threat and through threat we present purpose.

All the while, where opportunity presents itself, we are prepared to sprinkle yet even more vocabulary over children as they draw, not like a machine gun but sensitively. We seek the opportunities to comment on and draw attention to their drawings, to the details, to the possibilities, to the 'I wonder how . . . ?' or 'I wonder what . . . ?'. A third layer of language building on what we have already modelled.

And the last 3M, mathematics . . . ? Well, you can take a drawing anywhere mathematically. As we model our own drawing, we can drop in observational mathematics: combining numbers of fingers, counting buttons, drawing one more or one less of a feature, counting sticking up hair strands in twos, writing numerals on doors, giving characters numerals to eat, the list goes on. Drawing has a huge array of possibility for maths – passcodes are particularly engaging. Numerals that open doors, find treasure, release bats, turn characters into zombies, call witches – again, your imagination and the children's will be fertile ground for these.

If we have to 'teach' maths at a carpet time, then the mathematical skills from Drawing Club transfer seamlessly – children's confidence in representing their thinking pictorially emerges and we can explore problem solving with children drawing their ideas and in their own way. Again, the principle of threat and passcodes plays a big role – in some degree, it turns maths teaching into a story of its own. It opens up Maths World to children in a unique way, an extra layer over all the fabulous mathematical opportunities presented by your open-ended continuous provision.

In a way, drawings are like the continuous provision. You aren't planning them, but you are planning the 3Ms behind them. If you know your children's next steps, then each time they come to Drawing Club is an opportunity to 3M. The anythingness of their drawings presents the possibility for the anythingness of 3Ming. Their emotional connection drives them to want to respond to secret codes, or hidden messages, or passwords. We are in effect using drawing to bring the child's imagination 'out into the open' and then skilling them at the same time. In this moment, we are combining the world of play, the world of Story and the Adult World.

And what do they draw on? A4 paper normally does it or A5. Make it coloured paper if we wish to give choice. Avoid books wherever possible. If we can't and they are insisted on, then at least Drawing Club will retain the majority of its magic.

And what do we do with the pieces of paper? Well, I guess it's up to us. Stick them in a book, put them on the wall, offer them to the children to decide, take a photo, roll them up and hide them, send them home – whatever we feel we need to do or have to do. Come book scrutiny time, if these are insisted on, Drawing Club will blow them away so it'll be one less thing to worry about.

Muscle and Movement plays a huge role, too, by the way. With all its fine motor pencil control and tripod grip, Drawing Club gives children the opportunity to hold a pencil each day in a purposeful experience that they are invested in emotionally. To add the detail to drawing requires control and all the while we too are modelling grip in the comfort and intimacy of a small group of children – I've even found that children support one another in this too. They respect one another and guide one another on how to hold their pencils or how to add certain detail to their drawing. This experience builds on all the richness of the continuous provision and its resources which develop motor strength – yet again, another layer.

And the really clever bit? Children love drawing. It is in their DNA. Drawing is part of play. So each time they come to Drawing Club not only are we 3Ming, not only are we opening up the world of Story to them, we are also sprinkling skills that will enhance their play – it has a direct bridge to their world. It's why we find so many children doing their own Drawing Clubs. It's why we find parents asking what Drawing Club is because their children are doing it at home. Drawing is such a powerful precursor to 'writing', but in our hearts we also know it's a magic door to a place that is special beyond words: it's a door to the very soul.

CHAPTER 25

DRAWING CLUB AND THE MAGIC MIRROR

'New life, new love/Where's the heart I was dreaming of?/I need a new hope, new dream/Another heart in a different scene . . . '

– New Life, Pet Shop Boys

So, how does Drawing Club reflect in the Magic Mirror? If we are opening up the world of Story to children, is it adding to them or is it eroding them? We are introducing an 'adult-led' experience, so is it something that is only a 3 out of 10?

Let's take a look.

Choice

This is probably the most complex one to unpick. Children don't choose to come to Drawing Club. So, arguably, we are on to a zero straight away. It's true that they don't choose, but the 'why' underneath it validates them coming to it. We are opening a world of Story. We are giving them a 'hit' of 3Ms, we are developing fine motor skills. We are discovering more about them as people, as 'imaginators'. We are building on drawing that is a natural impulse for children to explore with. We are working with them for ten minutes per day – a fraction of their day. We are immersing them in an experience that soulifies.

We need to be sensitive to when we invite children to come to Drawing Club, mindful of their own play. Our initial input creates the conditions of choice – if we are offering an adventure, then children are more likely to want to join us. If we offer possibility, then children can bring 'themselves' to it. Ultimately, once they are in Drawing Club, there is choice – choice of what and how, with no right or wrong. It's why we adventure outside of the book, because we want it to be an experience of together-ness, each of us learning from the other. So, a point it is – 1 out of 10.

Creativity

This is almost certainly a point scored. We've already explored how drawing is a key form of self-expression, how when children draw, they are bringing images out of their minds and into reality. We are celebrating their inner worlds, we are valuing their interpretations and discovering their perceptions of what the world of Story might look like. True creativity is from the soul and when children draw, we are glimpsing this – we are privileged to share the moment with them, both the process and the product – 2 out of 10.

Curiosity

When we explore Story, when we present it as an adventure into another world that has a magic all of its own, then children's curiosity to discover more is triggered. If we enable them to want more, then they will. When we model and talk about our drawing, we reveal half a world, a world that they can bring themselves to because there is space for them to do so. If we are merely presenting 'draw this', then children have little wonder about what might happen as they draw. If we present the 3Ms just as 'write this', then there is no curiosity as to why we are writing – the message, the secret code, the password, the codes, the secret symbol that are part of the story that is unfolding before us, drive children to want to know 'what next?' For there to be curiosity, we need to present the Unknown and the world of Story can be just that – 3 out of 10.

Collaboration

Often when children work at tables there is silence as each child 'works' under the scrutiny of the adult. Drawing Club does away with this. We want talk. We want listening. We want ideas and critique and suggestions and the unfolding of story. That can never happen if we isolate each child, if drawing is merely a holding activity while children wait for their turn with the adult. We are having faith in children's capability. We are showing them that through solidarity and connection with one another good things can happen, that joy belongs in the social sphere. Now, of course, we are not 'making' children collaborate. We are, however, presenting its possibility – 4 out of 10.

Communication

As one of the main 3Ms, Making Conversation is integral to Drawing Club, which is why we are offering communication. In Drawing Club, language is being extended, introduced, reaffirmed, modelled, played with and shared. As children's drawings reveal themselves before us, we can take the art of communication in any direction we wish, whether it be nouns, synonyms, adjectives or sentence structure, each child in the Club being exposed to them on an equal footing. As you unearth new words together, it pays to send the children out into the continuous provision to literally go and 'spread the word'. And since children listen to children, they are far more likely to take all the richness in and return it to the Club or elsewhere within the provision through the power of Child Chat – 5 out of 10.

Core physicality

Another possibly contentious experience. We are sitting at a table. We aren't being hugely active at this point. However, it's for ten minutes maximum. We are sensitive to children's hodgepodge if they need to move around and the rest of our continuous provision is giving children ample opportunity to be physical and to take risk and to explore. In a way, Drawing Club is an exploration of our hand muscles – it's a physical adventure, but on a microcosmic scale. It is a hit of fine motor, of modelling, of control and, dare I say, it's a billion more times engaging than threading a teddy bear or going out of the room with a helpful, and yes, lovely grandparent to do some sewing – 6 out of 10.

Confidence

When children see that they can 'do' drawing, when they see that they are valued, that their time with you has been egalitarian with no control just adventure, when they feel the joy of Story, of having brought their imagination out of their brain, down their arm through their fingers and the pencil and on to the page where before there was nothing, when they see that their drawings are a message, a declaration of themselves, then two things happen: confidence goes upwards and you can give yourself another point – 7 out of 10.

Continuing progress

The progress children make is insane. There, I've said it. A bold claim, but you'll see it for yourself. A simple Drawing Club can be instrumental in bringing about huge progress. If we pitch the 3Ms at the cusp of understanding, if we have embraced play, if we commit to the adventure, then progress will come because, quite simply, it's almost impossible for it not to happen. Reluctant writers, the disconnected, boys, girls, our criers, our confident ones, our not so confident ones. Progress becomes unstoppable. Engage, excite, wonder, 3M and delight – the perfect conditions because Drawing Club thinks like a child and when we think like a child, we tune into what will motivate and what will make them think – 8 out of 10.

Commitment

This, then, is our commitment to Drawing Club – if we believe in it, if we have faith in children that is deep within us, if we are invested in bringing our own imagination to Drawing Club, then we can award a point. This should be the case to any 'teaching'. The profession of teacher is incredibly challenging – we are more and more institutionalised, we are leaving in droves, recruitment and retention are draining effectiveness of the system, the holidays never seem to be long enough by the time we have put ourselves back to pieces, the pressure to 'get' children to perform is immense, and many of our schools are living ghosts from the past, with all the absurdity and erosion of children they bring with them. So, if that's the case, why not two things that can bring you alive once more: play and Drawing Club? Both can resurrect us. It's what's needed – New Life – so why not reach out for it? – 9 out of 10.

Connection

Relationship is everything in education. In fact, love is everything in education. If children feel loved, if they feel special, if they are wanted and valued, then good things can happen. Drawing Club, like play, brings us into a shared magic where Story comes alive, where children thrive, where there is safety and bond in the book snuggle.

There is one other thing, the one thing that school is so good at evaporating and that is joy. When we have joy, when we see children glow, when they discover they are people not robots, it is in that moment that we can have real hope, a hope that can transform into faith and then lead to love.

It's the kind of love that can shape the soul for a lifetime so that one day, in a faraway summer, we might meet another soul who echoes us, whether it's a woman in a red dress with sunlight on her face or a man with a grey beard and a head full of dreams. They'll be out there, somewhere.

And it's for that reason that Drawing Club is 10 out of 10.

For examples of Drawing Club head to page 169.

CHAPTER 26

THE POSSIBILITY

'Nothing you say will ever be wrong/'Cause it just feels good being in your arms/And I'm running with you as fast as I can/Singing to myself I wanna hold your hand . . .'

– Downtown, Majical Cloudz

The two worlds, the world of the magic of children and the world of Story are all about possibility. Possibility comes from continuous provision that offers choice and autonomy. It comes from Drawing Club with all its richness and creativity.

They may seem separate entities, but in fact Drawing Club offers one possibility to play, and that is the possibility of immersion. I'm using the language of possibility because we are not insisting that children 'do' story in play. If we insist on this, then to a degree, we are eroding their ability to bring themselves to the provision, we are narrowing their horizons and maintaining control.

With Drawing Club we are 'suggesting'.

Let's take the example of *Not Now, Bernard*. Once the language, the story and the modelling have been shared, it is time for children to draw. Clearly, only six children will come initially, so the rest of the children will be heading into the landscape of the continuous provision. It's at this point that we suggest.

'You might want to go and make a trap to catch the monster . . . '

'You might want to build a new home for the monster in the garden . . . '

'You could make a monster detector in the creative area, so we know if the monster is on his way . . . '

'You might want to make a Lego telephone to call the police or you might want to be the police looking for the monster . . . '

We are scattering ideas that children might want to explore. Again, it comes back to thinking like a child. 'I have just heard a story about a monster, I am thinking that . . .' These ideas aren't challenges – they are not something to tick off. They are merely potential mini scaffolds for children to hang on to if they need to or want to.

We are leaving it open because we want to discover what it is the children are pursuing in their dream. We want to see how they will apply their skills in the provision – not the 'what' they do but more the 'how' and 'why'. If our provision is open-ended enough, then we will be witnessing wave after wave of autonomous problem solving, collaboration and thinkingness. Our suggestions act as mental provocations – some children will run with them; others will have a stronger dream or will want to wait until they join Drawing Club to reveal their 'story'.

Perhaps the biggest and most powerful possibility of Drawing Club is its ability to transition with the children when they leave Early Years. One of the reasons that I developed Drawing Club was that I have a dream for children to go through school being given the conditions for their essential selves to grow rather than be eroded. I wanted to try to reverse the tidal wave of wholeschoolism, to create something that the Magic Mirror would say 'yes' to and take it upwards, would take joy and love and emotional connection by the hand and follow the children.

If love can transform everything, then Drawing Club presents the possibility that education can be about joy, and that it can create the emotional connection to story that can echo upwards.

And so, if we can bring about a joy in Story, if we can shape children in their Early Years to see themselves as co-adventurers in our world of Story, then what reason would there be to shut the door to this once they leave Reception? Why would the Adult World present the world of Story in a dull and laborious way? If we are going to open up the wonderful world of Story, then we should be showing them the wonder.

The world of Story is a place that as adults we choose to reveal, so, are we truly going to set about eroding that one too by offering something dull and disconnected? Are we really going to erode the magic of children and the magic of Story at the same time? Are we going to be the destroyers of both worlds? Or are we going to delight in them both?

And the very best bit?

When we link Drawing Club with Play Projects, we discover that Early Years has a power, that it's time to stop defending and instead begin an even stronger advocacy of play and childhood. Because the power truly belongs in children and when Drawing Club and Play Projects are combined, we find that children have the opportunity to change the world, to change the future, to uncancel it and make it an index of possibility all for themselves.

PART 3

PLAY PROJECTS

CHAPTER 27

WHY PLAY PROJECTS?

'And when the answers only divide/When you never question the doubts in your mind/When the distance grows but the end is in sight/Nothing left to lose when there's nothing left to find . . . '

— *Something To Remember Me By*, The Horrors

Play is a conundrum to the Adult World. It doesn't train our mainstream teachers in it. It overlooks it in favour of formality, fed by accountability and the misconception that children can only learn in the presence of an adult, when they are being 'taught'. Because it's misunderstood, play gets sidelined. The Adult World separates it from learning and sees it as trivial, something that doesn't belong in school. Our school leaders and middle managers are most commonly teachers who are upper-school based – if they don't understand play, they don't look for it.

But what if there was a way to make play understandable? What if there was a way to reveal the magic of children so that the Adult World could open its eyes and see just what an effective tool play is for children? What if we could reveal the soul of children?

Well, we can. We can introduce a simple approach. It's called Play Projects. In essence, Play Projects is a framework that we put around play. The word 'play' is for children. The word 'projects' is for the adults. As soon as you call something a 'project', the Adult World starts to believe in it. It somehow validates it. What we're doing here is rebranding play to advocate play, to reveal it rather than have it closed down.

The word 'play' is critical to keep because we are sending a message about the importance of it – it's not 'challenge time' or 'learning time' or 'self-organised learning'. These phrases mean little to young children. They understand play, so we refer to it. We're not shy of play; we are proud advocates of it. We use Play Projects to come out in force, not hide away. The Adult World is obsessed with learning having to happen for every second of the day, with being able to see what is being learned so that it can monitor it and make children and teachers accountable – the Adult World demands learning. Because it finds play so inaccessible it shuts it down. So Play Projects act as a lens for this so that it can be 'seen'.

Play Projects are very much about the child's world. They act as a passport for the Adult World to glimpse the value of children's Seventh Sense, their magic and their soul. If we don't sing loudly about the power of play, then how will the Adult World ever know? How can it ever transform its worn-out view of what learning is and who children are? We are using Play Projects to forge a connection. We accept that the Adult World has forgotten how and why to play, so we use Play Projects to tell them.

Play Projects are the ultimate opportunity for the Seventh Sense to come to life and because of this they are 10 out of 10 in the Magic Mirror.

Choice

Children choose the 'subject' of their Play Projects for themselves and by themselves. They choose how they take shape and where they do them. Each Play Project is owned by the child. Play Projects are our declaration of faith – 'I trust you; I love you – play'. Choice is pivotal and the driving force.

Creativity

Since Play Projects embrace children's Seventh Sense, we cannot plan for them. They are the 'plan' of children. They are the interpretation of the landscape we provide. Since we don't know what each Play Project will be about, we cannot 'set up' provision. We just need to provide resources that are open-ended, that can be brought to life – we are offering the possibility that the world of things can be reimagined and repurposed. Each Play Project of itself is an act of creation.

Curiosity

Play Projects are not fixed in time. They can run for an afternoon. They can last for weeks. Each one is the energy and curiosity to explore and create further. A Play Project allows children to wonder and discover for themselves, to have those moments of realisation. They enable children to become conscious of their own innate power, of their own internal drive – they reveal the essential self so that it can be 'felt': through Play Projects, children become aware of themselves as autonomous learners. We are creating the conditions for self-curiosity.

Collaboration

Play Projects are individually chosen, but there are lots of occasions when children collaborate either on a shared idea or within one another's projects. They seem to respond to the idea that one another's play is important, that what they are doing has a value and therefore needs respect – they strengthen the solidarity of play even though the Play Projects are individually chosen. Differing confidences come together, supporting, challenging, questioning, enabling one another, problem solving and offering one another their Seventh Sense.

Communication

My Early Years colleague, Nic Lopez and I used to sit with the children at lunchtimes. It was a time to chat and share with children, enjoy their company rather than sit in the staff room and talk about mortgages and bills or relationships or holiday plans. What we discovered was that children were discussing what they were going to do in their Play Projects that afternoon. We knew then that communication was being enhanced by them and when the children immersed themselves in them, the language and discussion flowed out of them. Since each Play Project has its own focus, the possibilities of language become infinite – there are no Words of the Week here, there are no laminated signs because Play Projects are freedom and freedom takes language anywhere.

Core physicality

Play Projects can take place anywhere. Their physicality comes from the fact that children have free movement, inside, outside – they are not restricted. If our provision offers big-scale opportunities, then children are exercising the whole body – it's what play does after all.

Confidence

There is no greater feeling than doing something for yourself by yourself. When children become aware that the adults in the room have faith in them, when they sense that they are valued for their ideas and their 'whoness', then confidence blooms. Children become the authority, the leaders of the adventure, conscious of themselves and their importance. Play Projects empower children because they 'see' them.

Continuing Progress

As children take on their Play Project, our role as adults is to investigate the richness before us. We will want to explore the play that is unfolding in our environment. We will be intrigued. And as we adventure with the children, knowing their next steps, we sprinkle 3Ms over the top of interactions. As we do this, something extraordinary happens over time: children begin to 3M themselves – they begin to see that they can be independent, that they can move their own learning forward and that of their peers around them. Play Projects are the gift of learning autonomy.

Commitment

If we know that Play Projects are so powerful, then we will commit to them. If we know that they are independently chosen, then we can put greater energy into our Next Steps planning and exploring the fascinations and skills of children. We come alive to ourselves as educators. We are not bogged down by excessive planning because we can't plan what children will 'do'. The energy that children bring to their Play Projects rubs off on to us – it's the magic of children and its power to heal and to open up the adults to the transformative nature of play.

Connection

Play Projects connect us to children because they are playing. They are the world of children through a lens. If we are going to be an authentic co-adventurer, then we need authentic interactions and relationship. As children unfold before us, hope emerges, and since hope and faith lead to love, we discover a map into the unknown that has love at its heart. Play Projects nurture the essential self and there can be no greater love than that.

CHAPTER 28

THE BUILDING BLOCKS OF PLAY

'One day once when I had got some time/I tried to hold her, but she wouldn't be mine/She slipped through my fingers/And I missed the Mercury Girl . . .'

– *Mercury Girl*, Cleaners from Venus

Votre voix, vos yeux, vos mains, vos lèvres. Nos silences, nos mots. La lumière qui va, la lumière qui revient. Un seul sourire entre nous. En quête de connaissances, j'ai regardé la nuit créer le jour alors que nous semblions inchangés. O aimé de tous, aimé d'un seul, votre bouche a promis silencieusement d'être heureuse. Loin, loin, dit la haine; plus proche, plus proche, dit l'amour. Une caresse nous mène de notre enfance. De plus en plus, je vois la forme humaine comme un dialogue amoureux. Le coeur n'a qu'une bouche. Tout par hasard. Tous les mots sans pensée. Sentiments à la dérive. Les hommes errent dans la ville. Un coup d'oeil, un mot. Parce que je t'aime. Tout bouge. Nous devons avancer pour vivre. Visez tout droit vers ceux que vous aimez. Je suis allé vers toi, sans cesse vers la lumière. Si vous souriez, cela m'enveloppe d'autant mieux. Les rayons de tes bras percent la brume . . .

This is a quote from the film *Alphaville* by Jean-Luc Godard. It's beautiful, but unless you can read French, you won't understand it, you won't feel its beauty. We need to translate it to access it, to unfold it:

Your voice, your eyes, your hands, your lips. Our silences, our words. Light that goes, light that returns. A single smile between us. In quest of knowledge, I watched the night create day while we seemed unchanged. O beloved of all, beloved of one alone, your mouth silently promised to be happy. Away, away, says hate; closer, closer, says love. A caress leads us from our infancy. Increasingly I see the human form as a lover's dialogue. The heart has but one mouth. Everything by chance. All words without thought. Sentiments adrift. Men roam the city. A glance, a word. Because I love you. Everything moves. We must advance to live. Aim straight ahead toward those you love. I went toward you, endlessly toward the light. If you smile, it enfolds me all the better. The rays of your arms pierce the mist . . .

And in the same way, Play Projects translate the beauty of play through its framework. In essence, play is constructed of five main elements that we will make explicit to the Adult World:

- Building
- Creating
- Drawing
- Messaging
- Being.

Build

Children love to construct and make dens – Lego, building blocks, sticks, large cardboard boxes and bricks are just some of the things they like to build with. Small or big scale, creating spaces to hide in or act out in, building spaceships, castles, vehicles and towers are all things that children engage with. The scope for building is as infinite as a child's imagination.

Make and Create

Children's capability to make 'something out of nothing' is extraordinary. It's a channel for their Seventh Sense, being able to see the potential that lies in objects to become 'what-they-are-not'. When children make and create, they are revealing their soul – there is no predetermined adult outcome here – creativity comes right out from the child, transforming imagination into the tangible. It's astounding to witness what absorption and focus children are capable of once they get an idea in their head.

Draw

This is the link to Drawing Club. We already explored the great power of drawing and how children are naturally drawn to it, but now that we have confident drawers, we see an increase in independent engagement with it. Children begin to see that ideas can be drawn and that these are valued. Their ideas can be shared and explored collaboratively; they can be displayed for others to see and to be inspired by.

Message

If we have created the conditions for an effective Message Centre, then messaging will play an important role in children's play experiences. A Play Project will be ripe for messaging because there is always the sense within it that others need to know about it or that there is meaning to convey. Secret messages written on the things that children build or create is a highly engaging way of continuing the immersion in Mark Making.

Be

Pretending is a massive part of play. Acting out, role-playing, being someone other than oneself is a powerful way for children to create a narrative for themselves, to make sense of their role within the world and construct meaning. Pretending also gives children the possibility to democratically negotiate with one another, set boundaries, organise the 'what' and the 'how', and enter into a fantasy world with all its rich language and solidarity.

The framework doesn't alter play, it doesn't negate it. Instead, it accentuates it. It brings it into consciousness. For the children, it provides a context – to a degree, it gives them the insight into themselves as learners, empowering them to see the value of what they do and who they are. For the Adult World, Play Projects offer access to the magic of children. Even if the Adult World does not have faith, Play Projects give us hope that they can at least glimpse it and therefore value it.

And for one group of adults, Play Projects are extra powerful: parents. Parents don't necessarily understand play. They don't see it as 'learning' because the ghost from the past told them over and over that play is frivolous and not for school. Play Projects turn this on its head. Parents begin to see the power of play because their children will go home and talk about them – better still, if when you launch Play Projects you run a workshop for parents to come to. Children even ask to do Play Projects at home in the same way that they ask to do Drawing Club at home. Play starts to take hold in parental consciousness. The moment this starts to happen is the moment that the seeds are sown for change. We want parents to see the value of play so that they can question the diet of what their children are given in schools. If we accept that children need to be soulified, if we have hope that the current system that seems to destroy so much of children's essential self can be changed, then Early Years can have a significant ally in parents.

We want parents to become the advocates of play, too, and Play Projects give us a significant opportunity for play to follow children through school, just like a puppy dog called Eppie, my little shadow who happily trots along in the woods come what may.

CHAPTER 29

GETTING STARTED

'Sometimes I'm wondering under prehistoric skies/I feel it's all beginning right before my eyes/I must go back, re-examine my love . . . '

– *Lost*, The Church

When children play, they should be 'working' harder than you. Your role in Play Projects is twofold: to initiate the concept and then to 3M the play that unfolds before you. Once you get Play Projects underway and children understand that you are valuing their play, that it is important to you and to them, then in truth, the 3Ming becomes your main focus.

To get Play Projects we will model, in the same way that we do in Drawing Club. Children need to see the framework, so they get the sense that however their play evolves, you are co-adventuring with them and are intrigued to understand more.

To do this, we share a 'fake project' with them. The best time to introduce Play Projects is after lunch, but if you find a more effective time, then of course explore it. With all the children, you introduce your Play Project, drawing a large rectangle on the board and dividing it into four quarters.

In each quarter you write the different elements, but not 'being'. We exclude 'being' because we want to pretend play to emerge for itself and children will have far better ideas than we will on how to pretend.

In each quarter, we think out loud and 3M. Like this:

'My Play Project for today is going to be all about the Zoo. I went to the Zoo at the weekend so I'm going to explore it in my Play Project.'

'First, I'm going to go outside and **build** a brand new house for the lions because I think they need more room to walk around and I want them to be happy.' (We then draw a simple version of the lion house and 3M it – write a numeral on it, write a passcode or secret phrase.)

'Then I'm going to go to the Creative Area and I'm going to make a Zookeeper hat with paper and masking tape. I'm going to write a secret message inside it. I'll write it here; I wonder if you can read it?' (We draw the hat and write the secret message.)

'Then I'll go and draw some of the food I'll give to the lions if they are starving – "starving" means when we're really hungry and we just *have* to eat.' (I draw two things that the lions will eat and perhaps add chocolate buttons that we can count.)

'And then I'm going to go to the message centre and tell the Zoo Boss that I have made a new Lion House and we need more food.' (We model a short message.)

'That's my Play Project. I wonder what your Play Project is going to be? Close your eyes and count to ten.' (We count to ten.)

We then ask four confident children what they will do their Play Project on. They share their ideas. Sometimes we find that several children have the same Play Project in mind, so it can be a great opportunity to suggest collaboration.

And then, off they go!

It's as simple as that. We then go and immerse ourselves in their Play Projects – we become a co-adventurer in that very instant. I can't really tell you what will happen, because I've no idea. Neither do you. But the children will lead you into the unknown. They will show you themselves.

It's not only them that will grow in confidence. It is us. And our leaders. If they are confident, then so are we because we are embracing and demonstrating the power of play and the magic of children.

Play Projects aren't to be 'completed', by the way. The children aren't expected to go from one quarter to the next. They aren't challenge cards. If children say they have 'done' one of the quarters, we just ask, 'What next?'. We want Play Projects to emerge of their own will. It's why we 3M. If children are absorbed in building, then we ask to join in and 3M within that context. There is no 'you-have-to-do-this-ism', otherwise we are back to controlling again.

Some children, because they might lack confidence or need support, might not know what they want to do as a Play Project. This is where the Fake Project steps forward. We invite these children to join us – we turn the fake into reality. We suggest a collaboration and are able to model play in a closer context. We can also draw on the Play Projects of other children, asking them if the less confident children could help. Again, we are utilising the solidarity of play – the majority of children are only too happy to welcome others into their play.

Play Projects are the personification of the Golden Triangle: engaging environment, quality teaching and emotional connection. And the joy – well, that is on another level.

CHAPTER 30

CONTINUOUS PROVISION

'You could say I hear you on several high decibels/Over everything . . .'

– Over Everything, Courtney Barnett & Kurt Vile

I explored the necessity of open-ended continuous provision in *Can I Go and Play Now?'* so don't want to labour the point here particularly. To enable Play Projects, you need provision that is like a blank canvas – it has to be 'unintentional' because we don't know in what direction children are going to take their play. We can plan the types of resources that can be interpreted and that will lend themselves to physical development and the 3Ms, but their 'what-they-will-become' is unknown to us.

Examples of 'unintentional' continuous provision might look like the following.

Creative area

A range of materials to choose from, including junk modelling, various glues, paints, masking tape, hole punchers, staplers, string, paper, sticks, paper straws and anything that you can source that offers interpretation. If you are lucky enough to have a Scrapstore nearby, then make that a regular port of call – they are a rich source of often mind-blowing resources.

Block play

Block play and loose parts offer endless possibilities. They have no fixed outcome and can be explored in an infinite number of ways. It can often be effective to place some small world characters in here too, to hint at narrative. It's one of my favourite places within provision – the ways that children construct never ceases to amaze me and I usually leave there having unfolded some mystery.

Message centre

If we're going to have messaging as part of Play Projects, then we need a Message Centre. As we've already discovered, if we want to celebrate and encourage Mark Making, then let's make the process engaging and meaningful. We are assimilating Mark Making as part of play; we are giving it equal value. Messaging isn't a bolt-on, it's a central cog.

Role-play

Less is more when it comes to role-play and it's a good idea to have the Seventh Sense in mind when it comes to resourcing it. The more open-ended this space is, then the more we open the possibility to its 'anythingness'. If we set it up as a garden centre, then Play Projects will find it difficult to take hold in here. A role-play area doesn't have to be something to be something. In effect, it's about reimagining the continuous provision so that it enables children to bring themselves to it. After all, the magic lies in every child, not your beautifully curated garden centre.

For examples of Play Projects head to page 179.

CHAPTER 31

DEVELOPING PROJECTS

'She was from a movie scene/And now she plays in my head all day . . . '

– *1980s Horror Film*, Wallows

The Adult World is obsessed with making everything more complicated than it needs to be. It seems to find ways to turn the straightforward into a minefield. Play Projects are simple. The lens that Play Projects provides gives us simplicity. Play itself is actually very complex and that is its mystery to explore. The more we invest in Play Projects, the more we unearth, but the framework maintains its accessibility for all.

Yet we can develop Play Projects further if we wish. We can add further parts to them when we feel it appropriate, as children's sense of self emerges, as children move out of Reception and into KS1.

We can include the following.

Investigate

As Play Projects develop, we might decide to ask children what they know about their particular focus. We might share our own understanding. We make conversation. We add to one another's knowledge, we question and wonder together, we challenge each another and, if need be, we consult other sources such as books and the internet to find out more.

This brings an authenticity to research, to the use of non-fiction; it validates curiosity and sends the message to the children that the adult in the room is not the controller, the Knower. Investigating evolves as an act of collaboration, of equality, children sharing their developed understanding with one another and with us. Together we become a living network of knowledge.

Instruct

Sharing knowledge and new-found information, delighting in our achievements and the process we took to get there can be really powerful for children. An opportunity to present Play Projects at the end of the day can enable children to be respectful, be valued by one another and possibly most important, inspire them. When children see how others have applied their Seventh Sense, then this shares the magic among them – it spreads the idea of capability, of identity, of the power of the essential self. We give voice to children and if that's not a power in itself, then I don't know what is.

Collective

Sometimes the Adult World insists on themes or topics as part of the children's learning experience. Play Projects can be adapted around this, using its essence to do a 'collective Play Project'. The difference is that you are controlling the focus. Children would still have the opportunity to explore the continuous provision, but the project 'focus' has been chosen by the adult. Arguably, it won't be as engaging or as rich, but it will at least retain the 'flow' of children's experience and they can have choice as to whether they will build, make and create, draw, message, be or discover more. You might even consider running your topic for a shorter amount of time and then handing over certain sessions for children to do authentic Play Projects where they have full control again.

By keeping the framework of Play Projects within your topic, you at least retain the sense that children can explore it without sitting at a table cutting out pre-printed sheets to stick into a Science book, for example. It keeps the echo of autonomy and choice in spite of the focus being more controlled.

This echo offers the potential for Play Projects to follow children as they move through school, each year retaining elements of open-ended continuous provision and enabling sessions in which children can adventure, because change, however small it may be, is better than none at all. If continuous provision and the room for children to *be* follows with them from year to year, then the soul has been enabled to have greater space than it might do otherwise. We instigate the possibility for a reverse wholeschoolism, slowly opening the Adult World's eyes to the 'whoness' of children.

And just like Drawing Club, Play Projects can make the transition into Year 1. If we talk with our KS1 colleagues about the Magic Mirror, if we base our discussion around skills and share the Next Steps Planning, if we demonstrate how Drawing Club is an effective way to continue the adventure into Story and that it gives those who are unfamiliar with Next Steps Planning a chance to rehearse the use of the 3Ms and then take them into the continuous provision, if we show how Play Projects can engage and enable children to go deeper and further into their interests while still making progress that is 'viewable' by the Adult World, then it becomes a possibility.

And the possibility refracts into open-ended continuous provision going into Year 1. And if open-ended continuous provision goes into Year 1, then so does play. And if play goes into Year 1, then so does the Magic Mirror. And if the Magic Mirror goes into Year 1, so does the essential self. And if the essential self goes, so does the soul.

It's then that we have the possibility of beginning to turn the tide. It's then that we begin to show the power of play and the magic of children. It's then that we reveal delight in the soul. And if all this richness goes into Year 1 and the educators there begin to unfold their own understanding of children and what they are capable of, then don't we increase the possibilities of play and Drawing Club going into Year 2? And if we do that, then we begin to take the wider Adult World on the journey into the soul.

Because that's what this book has been all about. Yes, it's engaging Early Literacy, better pencil grips, effective transition, mathematics, outcomes, progress, play, greater language development, stronger boys' achievement, simpler planning, deeper interactions, the power of Story and closer emotional connection, but ultimately, it's about the soul and its adventure.

If Drawing Club and Play Projects enable the Adult World to see children in a new light so that it can see that they are capable, that they have a dream and that it is its duty to nourish and grow the soul, and that this can be embraced while progress follows, then we have begun change.

For when we discover the soul, we find love.

So, hold on to hope.

Keep faith.

Because if we do that, love will be on its way and it *will* change everything.

If You Don't Believe Your Dreams

And if you don't believe your dreams
Your heart cannot be broken
No pain to fade
No rain parade
At the close of your day.

And if you don't believe your dreams
You'll never be awoken
What may have been
Will stay unseen
As you go on your way.

But once in a faraway Summer
Once in blue moon say
You'll find a dream to hang on to
Don't let it slip away.

And if you do believe your dreams
Remember what they told you
Those ships go down
Those lovers drown
And you might lose it all.

And if you do believe your dreams
There's nothing here to hold you
But don't forget
No safety net
If you find that you fall.

Though once in a faraway summer
Once in blue moon say
You find a dream to hang on to
Don't let it get away . . .

(The Cleaners From Venus,
© Mr Mule, 2019)

PART 4

NOTES FROM

THE GREEN + BLACK BOOKS

"DON'T BE SATISFIED WITH STORIES,
HOW THINGS HAVE GONE FOR OTHERS.
UNFOLD YOUR OWN MYTH..." RUMI

WHO YOU
MIGHT BECOME
+ WHAT YOU
MIGHT DISCOVER

"IT IS NOT
DEATH THAT ONE
SHOULD FEAR,
BUT ONE SHOULD
FEAR NEVER
BEGINNING TO
LIVE..."
MARCUS AURELIUS

WHO YOU ARE
+ WHAT YOU KNOW

"WHERE THERE IS NO
HOPE, WE MUST INVENT
IT..." ALBERT CAMUS

NOTHING IS SET IN STONE

"WHAT WOULD LIFE BE IF WE HAD NO
COURAGE TO ATTEMPT ANYTHING?"
VAN GOGH

"TAKING A NEW STEP, UTTERING A
NEW WORD, IS WHAT PEOPLE FEAR MOST."
DOSTOEVSKY

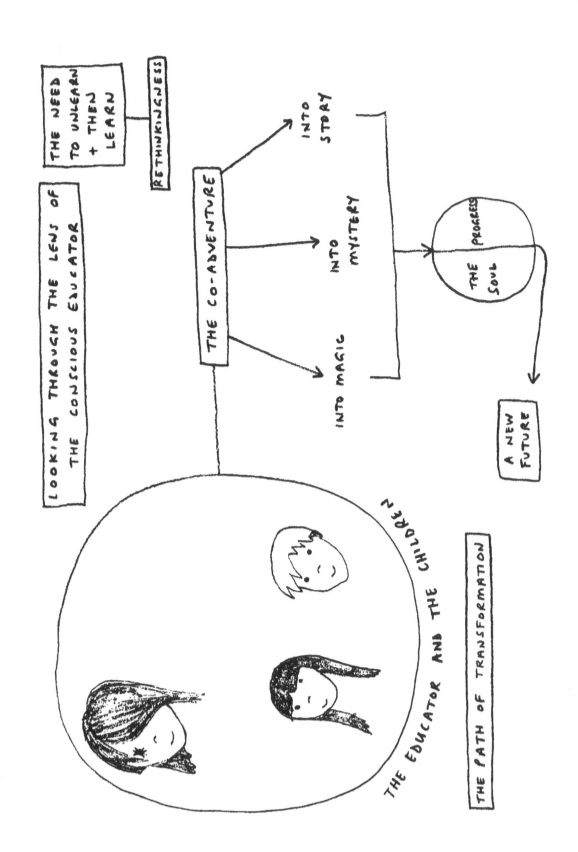

THE NEED TO UNLEARN + THEN LEARN

RETHINKINGNESS

LOOKING THROUGH THE LENS OF THE CONSCIOUS EDUCATOR

THE CO-ADVENTURE

INTO STORY

INTO MYSTERY

INTO MAGIC

THE PROGRESS SOUL

A NEW FUTURE

THE EDUCATOR AND THE CHILDREN

THE PATH OF TRANSFORMATION

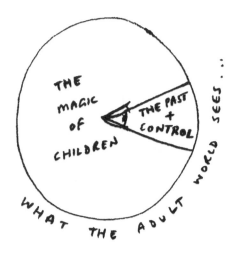

THE MAGIC OF CHILDREN

THE PAST + CONTROL

WHAT THE ADULT WORLD SEES ...

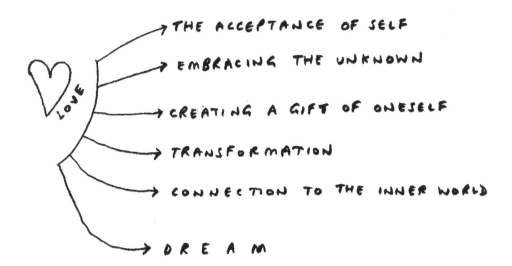

LOVE

→ THE ACCEPTANCE OF SELF

→ EMBRACING THE UNKNOWN

→ CREATING A GIFT OF ONESELF

→ TRANSFORMATION

→ CONNECTION TO THE INNER WORLD

→ D R E A M

WHEN WE PLAY + WHEN WE LOVE WE LOSE OUR SENSE OF TIME. WE BECOME ALIVE TO THE LITTLE THINGS + WE CONNECT TO OUR AUTHENTICITY.

CHILDREN HAVE THEIR OWN INTERNAL QUESTION.

THEY NEED TO EXPLORE + ADVENTURE TO
DISCOVER WHETHER THERE IS AN ANSWER
LYING IN WAIT

EXPECT THE
UNEXPECTED

SHAPING IDENTITY THROUGH THE LENS OF
CURIOSITY IN THE CONTEXT OF COMMUNITY

THE TRANSFORMATION OF THE OPAQUE INTO
THE TRANSPARENT : WHAT I DO NOT YET KNOW
CAN BECOME KNOWN, WHO I AM CAPABLE OF BEING
CAN COME INTO BEING-NESS.

THE ANSWER IS IN FRONT OF YOU

CURIOSITY IS THE WAY INTO THE WORLD...
CREATIVITY IS THE WAY TO CHANGE IT...
COMMUNICATION IS THE WAY TO SHARE THE DREAM...

IF YOU MEET
A WORKSHEET
ON THE ROAD,
KILL IT...

ANY THING CAN BE ANYTHING
ANY 'WHERE' CAN BE ANYWHERE

WONDER

IMAGINATION

PLAY IS NOT
A LUXURY...

WE FIND OURSELVES IN PLAY...
THROUGH JOY COMES NEW LIFE.

WHEN ADULTS PLAY THEY REPLACE THE
REMINDLESSNESS OF THEIR CHILDHOOD WITH
THE TIMELESSNESS OF CHILDHOOD.
PLAY IS A FORM OF <u>TIME TRAVEL</u>.

PLAY BRINGS THE WORLD TO LIGHT +
CREATES CONNECTION TO IT...

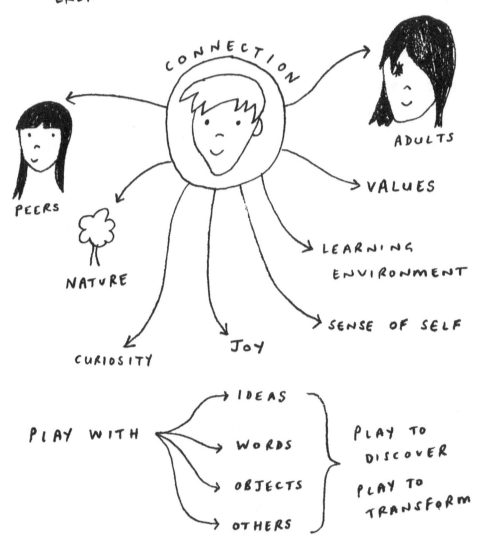

TO CREATE IS TO BRING SOMETHING
NEW INTO THE WORLD : LOVE , THINKING,
CONNECTION , SOUL AND EACH CREATION
IN ITS HEART HAS POTENTIAL TO TRANSFORM
THE WORLD INTO WHICH IT ENTERS...

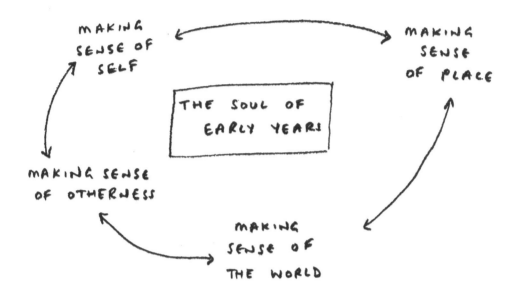

MAKING
SENSE OF
SELF

MAKING
SENSE
OF PLACE

THE SOUL OF
EARLY YEARS

MAKING SENSE
OF OTHERNESS

MAKING
SENSE OF
THE WORLD

THE UNKNOWN PLEASURES OF PLAY...
- ANYTHING THAT CAN BE
IMAGINED + ANYTHING THAT CAN
BE UNIMAGINED.

THE OBJECT SAYS "I AM WHAT I AM"
THE CHILD SAYS "BUT YOU ARE ALSO WHAT YOU
ARE NOT"

EVERY DAY, CHILDREN SHOW US A NEW WAY TO
SEE THE WORLD...

↳ THE CONSCIOUS EDUCATOR - I 'SEE' YOU

THE ADULT MUST BE CURIOUS TO UNEARTH
THE MYSTERY OF CHILDREN

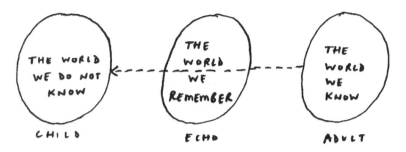

WE TAKE WHAT WE KNOW AND THE MEMORIES OF
OUR OWN CHILDHOOD INTO THE CHILDREN'S WORLD
TO NOT ONLY GLIMPSE MAGIC BUT IMMERSE
OURSELVES IN IT.

IF WE OFFER CHILDREN THE GIFT OF PLAY, THEY
WILL OFFER US THE GIFT OF MAGIC IN RETURN...

CHILDREN TAKE US ON A PILGRIMAGE
TO THE CENTRE OF THE SOUL: I WILL BE
FREE TO BECOME MYSELF.

THE ARCHITECTURE OF IDENTITY
I EXIST, I LIVE. I AM WHO I AM.

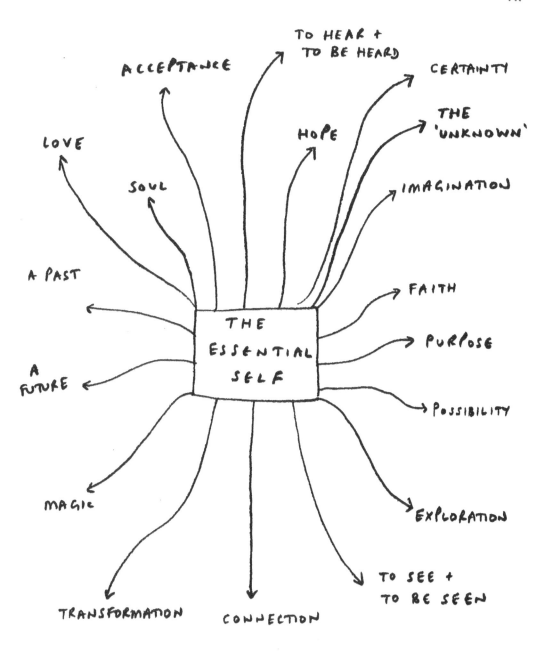

TO HEAR +
TO BE HEARD

ACCEPTANCE

CERTAINTY

THE
'UNKNOWN'

LOVE

HOPE

IMAGINATION

SOUL

THE
ESSENTIAL
SELF

A PAST

FAITH

PURPOSE

A
FUTURE

POSSIBILITY

MAGIC

EXPLORATION

TO SEE +
TO BE SEEN

TRANSFORMATION

CONNECTION

TO KNOW ONESELF IS TO BE ONESELF,

TO BE ONSELF IS TO LOVE ONESELF...

THE ESSENTIAL SELF IS THE INDEX OF POSSIBILITY
FOR THE FUTURE..

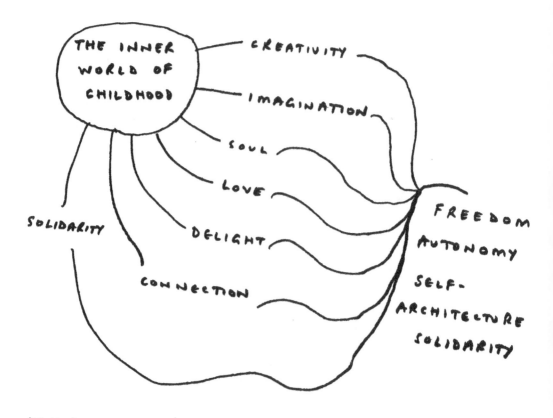

THE INNER WORLD OF CHILDHOOD

CREATIVITY

IMAGINATION

SOUL

LOVE

DELIGHT

CONNECTION

SOLIDARITY

FREEDOM
AUTONOMY
SELF-ARCHITECTURE
SOLIDARITY

WHAT DOES THE SOUL NEED TO TRULY FLOURISH?

L	O	V	E		
INSPIRATION		VITALITY		ACCEPTANCE	

THE INFINITE DAYDREAM OF THE SOUL...

THE SPIRAL

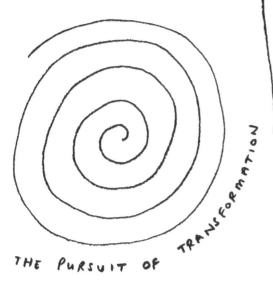

THE PURSUIT OF TRANSFORMATION

THE WORLD WE REMEMBER
THE WORLD WE KNOW
THE WORLD WE DON'T KNOW
INSIDE THE SPIRAL

TO TRAVEL, TO ADVENTURE THROUGH THE SPIRAL WE NEED OUR INNATE CURIOSITY, OUR NATURAL CREATIVITY + A STRENGTH OF SELF-PERCEPTION TO MEET ITS UNKNOWN AND HAVE THE POTENTIAL TO CHANGE IT.

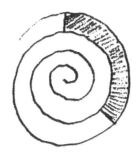

A NEO-LIBERALIST EDUCATION BLOCKS OR ERODES THE ESSENTIAL SELF - IT STEMS THE FLOW + CREATES DISCONNECTION FROM OUR AUTHENTIC SELVES.

WITH EACH STEP THROUGH THE SPIRAL, WE AWAKEN TO WHO WE ARE + WHO WE MIGHT BECOME...

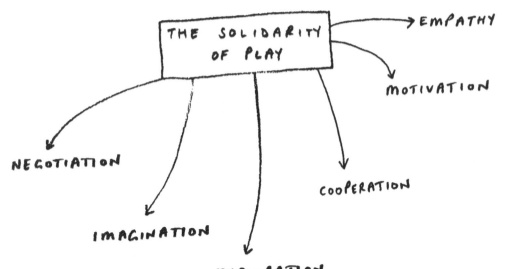

THE SOLIDARITY OF PLAY

→ EMPATHY

→ MOTIVATION

→ NEGOTIATION

→ IMAGINATION

→ COOPERATION

→ EXPLORATION

PLAY, WHEN IT PRESENTS RISK, ENABLES CHILDREN TO FEEL FEAR BUT PLAY WITH IT TOO. RESOLUTION THROUGH RISK SHAPES SELF-CONTROL AND A STRENGTH TO MEET THE UNKNOWN, . . .

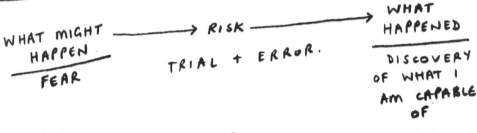

WHAT MIGHT HAPPEN / FEAR ——→ RISK ———→ WHAT HAPPENED

TRIAL + ERROR.

DISCOVERY OF WHAT I AM CAPABLE OF

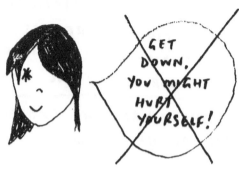

GET DOWN. YOU MIGHT HURT YOURSELF!

THE PROJECTION OF ADULT FEAR NEGATES THE POWER OF RISK AND THE EXPLORATION OF PHYISICALITY

THE ABILITY OF		
MY MIND	MY BODY	OTHERS

THROUGH SOLIDARITY WE
PROGRESS AS AN INVIDUAL...

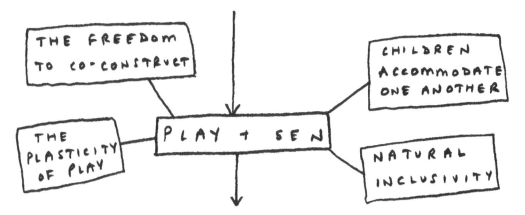

PLAY'S DEMOCRACY IS A GREAT
LEVELLER. CHILDREN SEE CHILDREN
NOT LABELS. THEY ARE CAPABLE
OF THE HIGHEST RESPECT + GREAT
LOVE FOR ONE ANOTHER. PLAY IS
WITHOUT PREJUDICE + THAT IS ITS
TRUEST POWER. IT SEES BEYOND +
OFFERS AN ADVENTURE THAT OPENS
ITS ARMS TO ALL...

WHEN PLAY IS IN THE AIR, CHILDREN
CAN LEARN ON THEIR OWN TERMS -
THEY ARE NO LONGER A 'WHAT-NESS',
INSTEAD THEY ARE A 'BEING-NESS'...

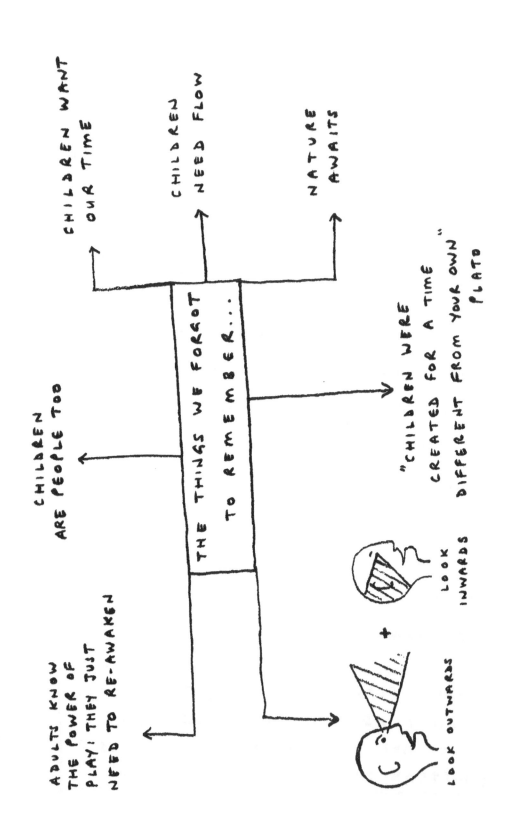

THE THINGS WE FORGOT TO REMEMBER...

CHILDREN WANT OUR TIME

CHILDREN NEED FLOW

NATURE AWAITS

CHILDREN ARE PEOPLE TOO

ADULTS KNOW THE POWER OF PLAY; THEY JUST NEED TO RE-AWAKEN

"CHILDREN WERE CREATED FOR A TIME DIFFERENT FROM YOUR OWN" PLATO

LOOK INWARDS

LOOK OUTWARDS

THE TAO OF PLAY:

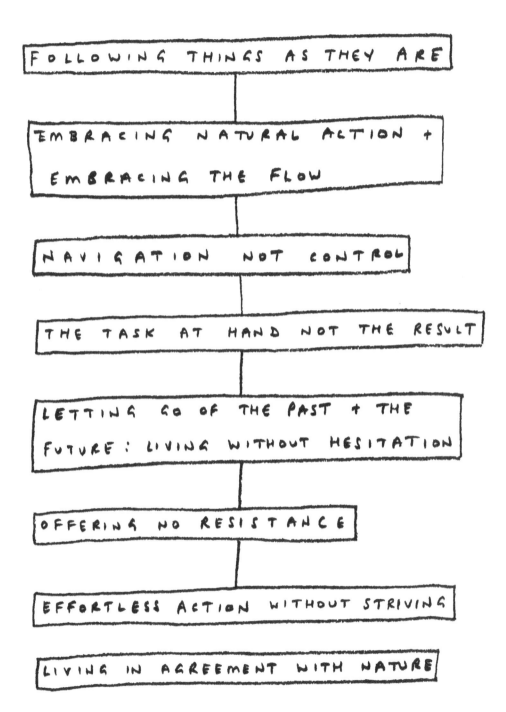

FOLLOWING THINGS AS THEY ARE

EMBRACING NATURAL ACTION + EMBRACING THE FLOW

NAVIGATION NOT CONTROL

THE TASK AT HAND NOT THE RESULT

LETTING GO OF THE PAST + THE FUTURE: LIVING WITHOUT HESITATION

OFFERING NO RESISTANCE

EFFORTLESS ACTION WITHOUT STRIVING

LIVING IN AGREEMENT WITH NATURE

ACTIVITY PLANNING

THE CHILD IS PULLED
TO KNOWLEDGE
INTO THE 'KNOWN'

NEXT STEPS PLANNING

THE CHILD + THE ADULT
ADVENTURE INTO THE UNKNOWN

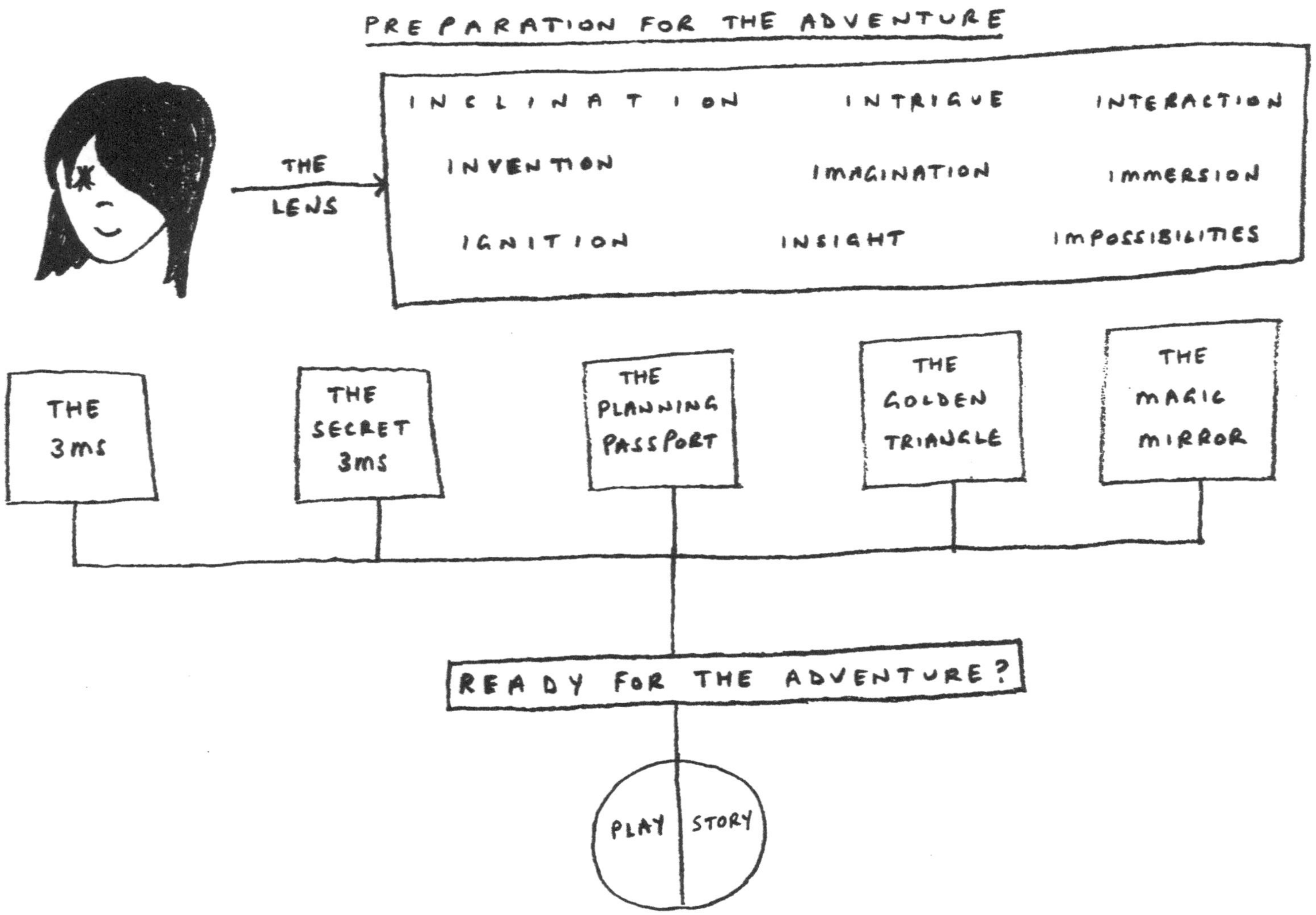

PREPARATION FOR THE ADVENTURE

INCLINATION	INTRIGUE	INTERACTION
INVENTION	IMAGINATION	IMMERSION
IGNITION	INSIGHT	IMPOSSIBILITIES

THE LENS

THE 3ms

THE SECRET 3ms

THE PLANNING PASSPORT

THE GOLDEN TRIANGLE

THE MAGIC MIRROR

READY FOR THE ADVENTURE?

PLAY STORY

THE MAGIC MIRROR IS POTENTIALLY
OUR EARLY YEARS TOOL FOR CHANGE:

'CAN THE ADULT WORLD DENY IT?
          TO DENY THE MAGIC MIRROR
IS TO DENY CHILDREN...

CHOICE   CREATIVITY   CURIOUSITY

CONFIDENCE   COLLABORATION   COMMUNICATION

CORE PHYSICALITY   CONTINUING   COMMITMENT
                     PROGRESS

                     CONNECTION

HOW MUCH IS REFLECTED IN EACH HOUR OF
THE SCHOOL DAY?

PARENTS SHOULD DEMAND MAGIC...

SHOULD CHILDREN DEMAND IT TOO..?

THE ADULT WORLD MAKES CHILDREN ACCOUNTABLE FOR THEIR
RESPONSES TO THE DIET IT GIVES THEM:
          PERHAPS THE CHILDREN SHOULD BEGIN
TO MAKE THE ADULT WORLD ACCOUNTABLE
IN RETURN...

THE MAGIC MIRROR

CHOICE ☐

CREATIVITY ☐

CURIOSITY ☐

CONFIDENCE ☐

COLLABORATION ☐

COMMUNICATION ☐

CORE PHYSICALITY ☐

CONTINUING PROGRESS ☐

COMMITMENT ☐

CONNECTION ☐

THE MAGIC MIRROR IS A TOOL OF
SELF-ASSESSMENT : HAVE WE ADDED TO
OR ERODED CHILDREN..?

158

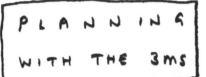
PLANNING WITH THE 3ms

YOU NO LONGER EXPLICITLY PLAN FOR CHILDREN'S DOING-NESS

YOU PLAN FOR YOUR ROLE AS THE ADULT, FOR THE LANDSCAPE TO ADVENTURE IN + FOR THE RICHNESS OF YOUR INTERACTIONS

YOU PLAN FOR YOUR DOING-NESS SO THAT CHILDREN CAN EXPERIENCE THEIR OWN BEING-NESS

THE WORLD ACCORDING TO MALCOLM + JOYCE:

"IF YOU THINK ABOUT IT, PLAY IS ALL ABOUT COLLABORATING + ROLE PLAYING - SOMETIMES YOU LEAD, SOMETIMES YOU FOLLOW. YOU LEARN HOW TO ADAPT + YOU DISCOVER YOUR ABILITY TO MAKE THINGS HAPPEN. PLAY MEANS THAT IF SOMETHING YOU ARE DOING TOGETHER FAILS, THEN YOU FAIL TOGETHER + ONE OF YOU WILL HAVE THE SOLUTION...."

THE 3M I OVERLOOKED....

MAKING FRIENDS

LISTENING

TURN TAKING

EMPATHY

NEGOTIATION

COLLABORATION

YOU-NESS

LOVE

ME-NESS

CONNECTION

SUPPORTING

SOLIDARITY

PLAYING A ROLE

RESPECT

INSPIRATION

PLANNING

HOW TO 3m

LOOK:

WHAT PLACES ARE THERE
TO HIDE MESSAGES?

WHAT OPPORTUNITIES ARE
THERE FOR MATHEMATICS?

DO THE CHILDREN NEED ME
AT THIS POINT?

WHAT ARE THE CHILDREN
TELLING ME ABOUT THE
SPACE + THE RESOURCES?

LISTEN:

WHAT CONVERSATION
IS HAPPENING?

WHAT OPPORTUNITIES ARE
THERE TO SPRINKLE +
REPEAT VOCABULARY?

WHAT OPPORTUNITIES ARE
THERE TO MODEL
CONVERSATION + TALK?

ACT:

"I WONDER WHAT WOULD HAPPEN IF WE...?"

"I'VE GOT A GREAT IDEA, I'LL NEED A PENCIL +
PAPER + I'LL SHOW YOU..."

"I BET YOU CAN'T..."

"THERE'S NO WAY YOU'LL BE ABLE TO DO..."

"WHO HERE THINKS THEY CAN...?"

"HOW DID YOU DO THAT...?"

"IS THERE ANOTHER WAY TO...?"

"LOOK AT THIS, I DID..." [YOU MAKE SOMETHING
LIKE A LITTLE TOWER + TELL
THE CHILDREN NO ONE CAN
BUILD TALLER]

THE HORIZON LEANS FORWARD...

THE HIDDEN ART OF 3ms

+ THE HIDDEN ART OF DRAWING CLUB
    + PLAY PROJECTS

CHILDREN SHAPE THEIR ESSENTIAL SELVES	THE ADULT WORLD GETS ITS PROGRESS

THE MAGIC MIRROR

WE PLAN FOR SKILLS....

WE SOULIFY CHILDREN

THE DEMANDS OF THE ADULT WORLD ARE NOT IMPOSSIBLE TO CHANGE, BUT THEY ARE INACCESSIBLE FOR THE MAJORITY TO DO SO. IF WE TRANSFORM HOW WE MEET THE DEMAND, THEN WE MAKE A CHANGE... A CHANGE THAT ADDS TO CHILDREN RATHER THAN ERODING THEM.

CONTINUOUS PROVISION : KEY COMPONENTS

LOOSE PARTS   'LEGO CLUB'   SAND
- BIG SCALE   - CHECK TOM BEDARD

                                        COOKERY
                                        - FRESH BREAD

WOODWORKING STATION   SELF SERVE SNACK
- CHECK PETE MOORHOUSE   - INDEPENDENCE
                                        - CHOICE
            ┌─────────┐
            │ OPEN   │   CONSTRUCTION
TINKER TABLE│ ENDED   │   - MIX IT UP
-           └─────────┘

                                        SMALL WORLD
MESSAGE CENTRE
                              ┌──────────────────────────────┐
                              │ THINKING OF HAVING AN   │
LARGE SCALE WATER   │ EXPLICIT MATHS ZONE ? WHAT   │
- DRAIN PIPES   - BUCKETS   │ IS THE IMPLICIT MESSAGE TO   │
- WHISKS   - TURKEY BASTERS │ THE CHILDREN ? IS MATHS   │
- CHECK TOM BEDARD   │ CONFINABLE ?   │
                              └──────────────────────────────┘

┌──┐
│ DIE FRÖHLICHE WISSENSCHAFT...   │
│ THE JOYFUL PURSUIT OF KNOWLEDGE + UNDERSTANDING   │
└──┘

THE ART OF SECRET SYMBOLS

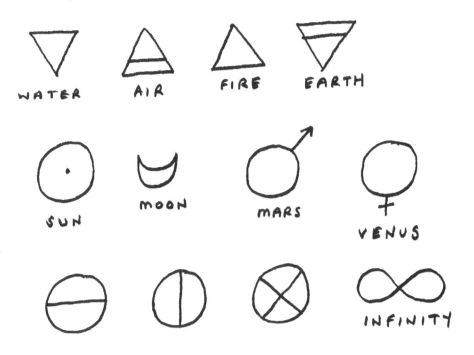

WATER   AIR   FIRE   EARTH

SUN   MOON   MARS   VENUS

INFINITY

ELEMENTAL + PLANETARY SYMBOLS:

NO 'RIGHT' WAY

NO DEFINED MEANINGS

CHILDREN CREATE
THEIR OWN

PROTECTION

WATER HOUSE

NATIVE
AMERICAN
SYMBOLS

DAYS + NIGHTS

RAIN

RUNES AS SECRET SYMBOLS

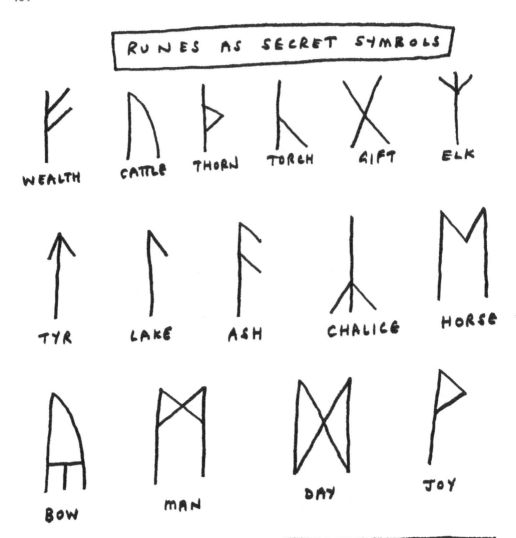

WEALTH   CATTLE   THORN   TORCH   GIFT   ELK

TYR   LAKE   ASH   CHALICE   HORSE

BOW   MAN   DAY   JOY

AS WITH ALL SECRET SYMBOLS, THERE IS NO 'RIGHT' + MEANING IS NOT FIXED. SYMBOLS ARE FOR PLAYING WITH AS IS WHAT THEY SIGNIFY...

THE 'TRICK' OF DRAWING CLUB + PLAY PROJECTS

DRAWING CLUB + PLAY PROJECTS ARE CENTRED AROUND CREATIVITY, <u>SKILLS</u>, IMAGINATION + A SHIFT IN HOW WE VIEW 'TEACHING!

BOTH RELY ON OPEN-ENDED CONTINUOUS PROVISION, FREEDOMS, CHOICE, EQUALITY.

PLAY, DRAWING CLUB + PLAY PROJECTS MOVE CHILDREN FORWARD - WE ARE MAKING PROGRESS EXPLICIT WITH A FRAMEWORK.

IN TRANSITION, WE HAVE A STRONGER FOOTHOLD BECAUSE IT IS CLEARER FOR THE ADULT WORLD TO SEE THE POWER OF PLAY + SKILLS BASED NEXT STEPS PLANNING.

THEY INCREASE THE POSSIBILITY FOR CONTINUOUS PROVISION TO MOVE UP WITH THE CHILDREN - LOOSE PARTS, A CREATIVE AREA, A MESSAGE CENTRE + A CONSTRUCTION AREA <u>CAN</u> ECHO IN EVERY CLASSROOM...

THE PARALLEL WORLDS...

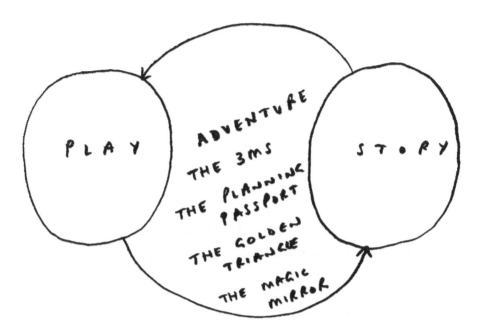

PLAY

STORY

ADVENTURE
THE 3MS
THE PLANNING
PASSPORT
THE GOLDEN
TRIANGLE
THE MAGIC
MIRROR

THE WORLD OF PLAY	THE WORLD OF STORY

ADVENTURE

ANYTHING CAN BE IMAGINED

ANYTHING CAN HAPPEN

MALEVOLENCE CAN BE OVERCOME

CONNECTION

UNFOLDING-NESS

A NEW WAY TO SEE THE WORLD

EMPATHY + SOLIDARITY

TIMELESSNESS

JOY

SHARING IN STORIES + PLAY...

WHEN WE SHARE STORIES + WHEN WE ENABLE PLAY THEN WE WITNESS THE EXTRAORDINARY. WE SEE THE POWER OF IMAGINATION, THE ART OF INVENTION + THE COMMUNITY OF THINKERS, DOERS + DREAMERS BEFORE US.

CHILDREN ARE CAPABLE. THEY CAN MAKE CHOICES. THEY CAN PLAN. THEY CAN CREATE + NEGOTIATE + TAKE RISKS + CARE FOR ONE ANOTHER.

CHILDREN NEED DEMOCRACY NOT TYRANNY.
CHILDREN NEED SPACE TO 'BE'.
CHILDREN NEED TO BE VALUED FOR THEIR 'WHO-NESS'
CHILDREN NEED LOVE.

STORIES ARE A WAY. TO MAKE WHAT SEEMS IMPOSSIBLE BE POSSIBLE...

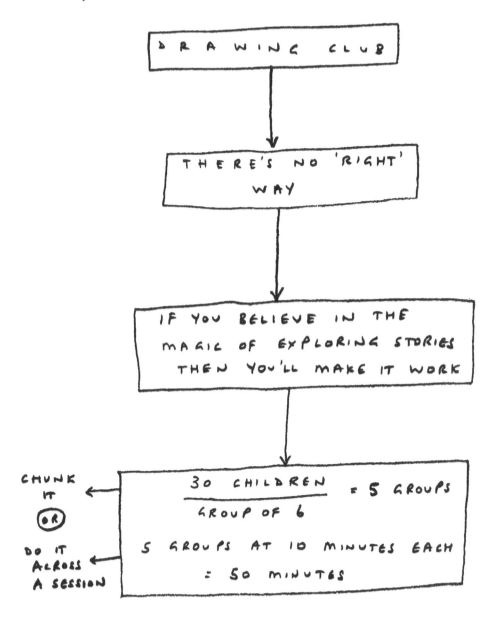

DRAWING CLUB

↓

THERE'S NO 'RIGHT' WAY

↓

IF YOU BELIEVE IN THE MAGIC OF EXPLORING STORIES THEN YOU'LL MAKE IT WORK

↓

$$\frac{30 \text{ CHILDREN}}{\text{GROUP OF } 6} = 5 \text{ GROUPS}$$

5 GROUPS AT 10 MINUTES EACH = 50 MINUTES

CHUNK IT ←

(OR)

DO IT ACROSS A SESSION ←

IF CHILDREN GO + DO THEIR OWN DRAWING CLUB, THEN 3m THEIR DRAWINGS - DON'T 'MAKE' THEM DO IT AGAIN WITH YOU...

DRAWING CLUB - WEEKLY STRUCTURE

MONDAY	TUESDAY	WEDNESDAY	THURSDAY	FRIDAY
CHARACTER	SETTING		ADVENTURE WITH THE STORY	

IMAGINING   POSSIBILITY   LOOKING

SHARING THINKING   WONDERING   RE-IMAGINING

EXPLORING   SHARING KNOWLEDGE

D R A W I N G   C L U B

W E D N E S D A Y — F R I D A Y   A D V E N T U R I N G

P O S S I B I L I T I E S

F O O D

- TREATS
- TRICKS
- POTIONS
- INGREDIENTS
- COMBINATIONS

P L A C E S

- HIDE-OUTS
- BASES
- PLANETS
- HOUSES
- MAPS
- BEDROOMS

C H A R A C T E R S

- FAMILY
- ALIENS
- MONSTERS
- ANIMALS
- RESCUERS

M A L E V O L E N C E

- THINGS FALL OFF
- FALL DOWN HOLES
- GET LOST
- GET STUCK
- CAN'T MOVE
- TRAPS

T R A N S F O R M A T I O N

- TURN INTO NEW CHARACTER
- DECIDE DIFFERENTLY
- FIND SOMETHING THAT WILL HELP
- MACHINES + INVENTIONS

M A G I C

- SOMETHING KOOKY HAPPENS
- SOMETHING KOOKY APPEARS
- SOMETHING DISAPPEARS
- SPECIAL POWERS

V E H I C L E S

- ESCAPE
- MOVE FASTER
- GO IN TO SPACE
- GO UNDERGROUND
- TAKE PASSENGERS
- FLY
- TRANSPORT

DRAWING CLUB

SHARING STORIES:

ON AVERAGE THERE 39 SCHOOL WEEKS IN A YEAR.

YOU MAY WANT TO EXPLORE DRAWING CLUB JUST FOR A TERM. YOU MAY WANT TO EXPLORE IT FOR 30 WEEKS. IF SO, YOU NEED 10 STORIES, 10 BOOKS + TEN 'TIME OF A JOINT' CARTOONS.

HERE ARE THREE OF EACH TO GET YOU STARTED...

STORIES	BOOKS	TIME OUT OF JOINT
THREE LITTLE PIGS	NOT NOW BERNARD BY DAVID MCKEE	WACKY RACES
LITTLE RED RIDING HOOD	A DARK DARK TALE BY RUTH BROWN	PINK PANTHER
THE MAGIC PORRIDGE POT	WHAT'S IN THE WITCH'S KITCHEN BY NICK SHARRATT	ROAD RUNNER

DRAWING CLUB

NOT NOW BERNARD - EXAMPLE

MODELLED DRAWING + DRAWING CLUB

MONDAY	TUESDAY	WEDNESDAY	THURSDAY	FRIDAY
CHARACTER	SETTING	VEHICLE	MALEVOLENCE	PLACE
MONSTER	BERNARD'S HOUSE	PARENTS ESCAPE	PARENTS MEET EVEN BIGGER MONSTER	PARENTS HIDE

THE ACT OF PLANNING BECOMES AN ACT OF CREATION. IT BECOMES AN ACT OF STORYTELLING. SIMPLICITY OPENS THE DOOR TO IMAGINATION. YOUR MODELLED DRAWING IS NOT THE EXPECTED RESULT. YOU DO NOT KNOW WHAT THE CHILDREN WILL DRAW - YOU ONLY KNOW THE NEXT STEP: SKILL THAT YOU WILL SPRINKLE.

DRAWING CLUB

3 LITTLE PIGS - EXAMPLE

MODELLED DRAWING + DRAWING CLUB

MONDAY	TUESDAY	WEDNESDAY	THURSDAY	FRIDAY
CHARACTER	SETTING	FOOD	TRANSFORMATION	MAGIC
TEAM PIG OR TEAM WOLF?	PIG'S BRICK HOUSE	WHAT MACHINE COULD WE INVENT TO MAKE WOLF BURGERS?	THE PIGS ATE WOLF BURGERS BUT TURNED INTO SCARY ANIMALS...	WHO CAN COME + SAVE US?

INVENTIONS + MACHINES INTRODUCE 'HOW THINGS WORK' + ADDS A LAYER OF THE EXTRAORDINARY. CHILDREN OFTEN GO + MAKE THEM.

DRAWING CLUB

WACKY RACES

MODELLED DRAWING + DRAWING CLUB

MONDAY	TUESDAY	WEDNESDAY	THURSDAY	FRIDAY
CHARACTER	SETTING	MALEVOLENCE	MAGIC	PLACES
TEAM PENELOPE OR TEAM DASTARDLY?	VEHICLE THAT CAN WIN THE RACE	TRAP TO STOP OTHER VEHICLES	WHAT WOULD BE FIRST PRIZE? WHAT WOULD THE LOSERS GET?	MAP OF THE RACE TRACK

PLANNING EACH DAY REQUIRES YOU TO MAKE CONNECTIONS + EXPLORE THE EXTRAORDINARY. IN A WAY, IT IS RE-CONNECTING YOU TO YOUR OWN 'SEVENTH SENSE': HOW CAN I RE-IMAGINE THE WORLD? WHAT ARE THE POSSIBILITIES?

D R A W I N G   C L U B

THE STRUCTURE

1	INTRODUCE 6-8 WORDS
2	SHARE 'STORY'
3	MODEL DRAWING + 3M IT
4	DRAWING CLUB

- ONE 'STORY' PER WEEK (IF YOU THINK A STORY HAS STRETCH POTENTIAL THEN GO FOR IT!)

- STEPS 1-3 SHOULD BE AROUND 10-15 MINUTES MAXIMUM

- STEP 3 SPRINKLES 3ms OVER YOUR DRAWING. BRING CHILDREN'S ATTENTION TO THE DETAIL YOU ARE ADDING

- DRAWING CLUB IS MOST EFFECTIVE IF EACH CHILD EXPERIENCES IT EVERY DAY.

- AS EACH CHILD 'FINISHES', INVITE ANOTHER CHILD - REMEMBER TO LOOK FOR THE BEST OPPORTUNITY

- DON'T GROUP THE CHILDREN

EXAMPLE OF MODELLED DRAWING

"HE LIKES TO EAT WORD ICE CREAM PUDDING, HE'LL EAT THESE WORDS TODAY..." [MODEL WRITING]

"HE'S GOT TWO BEADY EYES"

"HE'S HAPPY BECAUSE HE'S GOING TO GOBBLE UP A TEACHER"

"MY MONSTER HAS TWO SHARP TEETH THAT POINT UPWARDS!"

4

"HE HAS FOUR BUTTONS. I'LL WRITE THE NUMERAL 4 LOOK HOW I DO IT., ITS ALL STRAIGHT LINES."

"I'LL DRAW A POCKET ON HIS SHORTS. I WONDER WHAT A MONSTER KEEPS IN HIS POCKET?"

"HIS SHORTS' ARE RIPPED SO I'LL DRAW ZIG ZAGS."

"HE HAS THREE CLAWS ON ONE FOOT + THREE ON THE OTHER. THAT'S SIX ALTOGETHER!"

DRAWING CLUB + THE 3ms

MAKING CONVERSATION

AS CHILDREN DRAW, WONDER OUT LOUD ABOUT WHAT DETAIL THEY MIGHT INCLUDE. BE CURIOUS ABOUT THEIR IMAGINATION. SPRINKLE VOCABULARY.

AVOID 'ADDING VALUE' E.G. DON'T TELL CHILDREN THEY ARE GOOD AT IT.

MARK MAKING

- USE THE POWER OF SECRETS + MESSAGING

- CHILDREN WRITE WHAT IS PURPOSEFUL FOR THEIR DRAWING

- ASK BEFORE YOU MAKE ANY MARKS E.G. YOU WRITE A SECRET FOR THEM TO READ. IT IS THEIR PICTURE.

- JOY COMES THROUGH IMAGINING THE KOOKY + THE STRANGE. A SECRET WORD OR SENTENCE DOESN'T HAVE TO BE 'ABOUT' THE DRAWING. IT'S 100% ABOUT THE NEXT STEPS OF THE CHILDREN

MATHEMATICS

- ALL DRAWINGS HAVE POTENTIAL FOR MATHS WITHIN THEM.

- PASSCODES, COUNTING, COMBINING, SUBTRACTION, NUMERALS, SIZE, SHAPE, COMPARISON AND ON + ON!

SUPER HEROES

BUILD

17 12 20

"I'm going to build a secret base + it has a passcode to get in — I bet you don't know it!"

DRAW

"He's got one more than two buttons"

"I'm going to draw an evil robot to defeat. Defeat means to beat someone."

MAKE + CREATE

F △ ▽

"I'm going to make some power bands + write a secret symbol inside them so they can make me invisible...."

MESSAGE

Help us Batman !

"I've put an exclamation mark at the end. That could be a secret symbol!"

"I'm going to send a message to Batman so he can come + help..."

PLAY PROJECTS

CHICKENS

BUILD

"I'VE USED SEVEN
BLOCKS. I WONDER
WHAT ONE MORE
THAN SEVEN IS ?"

"I'M GOING TO GO OUTSIDE + BUILD A
CHICKEN CASTLE TO KEEP MY
CHICKENS SAFE FROM MR WOLF...."

DRAW

17 14 11 9

"THIS IS HER PHONE
NUMBER"

"I'M GOING TO DRAW SUPER CHICKEN
SHE WILL COME + RESCUE THE OTHER
CHICKENS IF MR WOLF COMES"

MAKE + CREATE

beep
boop

"I'M GOING TO MAKE A WOLF DETECTOR.
IT WILL SAY, 'BEEP BOOP' IF THE WOLF
COMES. LETS WRITE 'BEEP BOOP' SO THE
CHICKENS KNOW WHAT TO LISTEN FOR."

MESSAGE

We will put you in the
bin !

"I'M GOING TO WARN MR WOLF
NOT TO COME. I WONDER IF WE
HAVE A BIN BIG ENOUGH ?"

BIRTHDAYS

BUILD

"I'M GOING TO BUILD SEVEN PARTY TOWERS IN THE CONSTRUCTION AREA. HAVE I BUILT ENOUGH?"

"I WONDER WHAT A PARTY TOWER IS?"

MAKE + CREATE

pepperoni pizza

"I'M GOING TO MAKE PIZZAS IN THE PLAYDOUGH. TO HAVE A BITE YOU HAVE TO READ THE SECRET PASSWORD. ISN'T 'PIZZA' A FUNNY LOOKING WORD?'"

DRAW

"I'M GOING TO DRAW THE PEOPLE WHO ARE COMING TO MY PARTY. IT'S A STRIPY PARTY. I WONDER IF A TIGER COULD COME? COULD A CAT?"

MESSAGE

Cats can come to the party.

"MY CAT HAS STRIPES SO I WILL WRITE A MESSAGE TO HIM – LET'S WRITE IT TOGETHER – I'LL NEED YOUR HELP!"

COLLECTIVE PLAY PROJECT

IF YOU **HAVE** TO DO A TOPIC
DO YOU NEED TO DO IT TO DEATH?

ALL YOU DO IS THINK, THINK, THINK... LIKE THIS

CLIMBING

PLANTING NURSERY

CHAIN SAWS

PLANTING MACHINERY

ANIMALS

FUNGUS

AXES

RINGS

TWIGS

RECYCLING

FRUIT

FALLING

TIMBER LORRIES

KEEP OUT SIGNS

WOODWORK

TREE-HOUSE

GO OUTSIDE

SHADE

NUTS

FANTASY TREES

HARD HATS

TREES

LEAVES

SHELTER

ROPES

NESTS

BARK

MAPS

INSIDE

ROOTS

HEIGHT

SWINGS

LOGGING

SEEDS

PLANKS

NOW BUILD, MAKE + CREATE, DRAW, MESSAGE, BE, INVESTIGATE, DISCOVER MORE...

THE WORLD ACCORDING TO MALCOLM + JOYCE...

"LOTS OF CHILDREN DON'T GET TO PLAY ANYMORE. IT'S SAD..."

"PLAY IS HOW CHILDREN LEARN..."

"IT'S LIKE GROWN UPS LIVE IN A TINY WORLD, AND CHILDREN LIVE IN AN INFINITE ONE..."

"CHILDREN HAVE JUST GOT SOMETHING ABOUT THEM..."

MALCOLM + JOYCE ARE IN THEIR 70s. THEY HAVE NEVER BEEN TEACHERS. THEY ARE FAMILY FRIENDS - WHEN THEY ASKED ABOUT THIS BOOK THIS IS WHAT THEY SAID WHILE I SIPPED TEA....

"IT'S LIKE CHILDREN ARE AWAKE TO THE WORLD..."

"CHILDREN HAVE LOTS TO TEACH US. WE JUST NEED TO LISTEN."

"LOOK FOR PEOPLE WHO INSPIRE YOU + SPEND MORE TIME WITH THEM."

"SPEND TIME WITH DOGS + CHILDREN. THEY ARE WHERE THE GOOD THINGS ARE..."

"REALLY, THE ADULTS NEED TO UNLEARN..."

"YOU GO OUT AT NIGHT + LOOK UP AT ALL THE GALAXIES + REALISE JUST HOW SMALL YOU ARE..."

"IF SCHOOLS SPENT THE TIME DOING TESTS ON PLAYING, THE WORLD WOULD BE VERY DIFFERENT..."

"QUESTION EVERYTHING"

"CHILDREN WILL LOOK FOR PLAY, IT'S WHO THEY ARE"

FURTHER READING + LISTENING

THOMAS HARDY 'RETURN OF THE NATIVE'

MARK FISHER 'GHOSTS OF MY LIFE'

HARUKI MURAKAMI

NICK DRAKE

THE LILAC TIME RETURN TO YESTERDAY

EDD DONOVAN + THE WANDERING MOLES

PHILIP K DICK 'DO ANDROIDS DREAM OF ELECTRIC SHEEP?'

ALAN WATTS 'ON THE TABOO AGAINST KNOWING WHO YOU ARE'

FUNERAL ADVANTAGE

AUGIE MARCH 'AFTER THE CRACK UP'

DAVID SYLVIAN SECRETS OF THE BEEHIVE

LUDWIG WITTGENSTEIN THE BLUE + BROWN BOOKS

DONNIE DARKO

J. D. SALINGER THE CATCHER IN THE RYE

F. SCOTT FITZGERALD THE GREAT GATSBY

LOST IN TRANSLATION

HERMANN HESSE STEPPENWOLF

FLOWERS

FRANZ KAFKA

PREFAB SPROUT

NIETZSCHE BEYOND GOOD + EVIL

THE MARY ONETTES

JEAN-LUC GODARD BREATHLESS

THE CURE DISINTEGRATION

JACK KEROUAC DESOLATION ANGELS

CARL JUNG

JOHN KEATS

THE GO-BETWEENS

HENRY MILLER TROPIC OF CANCER

TOURISTS ALL WE DO IS PRETEND

MARK EITZEL

MICHEL FOUCOULT THE ORDER OF THINGS

ROBERT FORSTER

DAVID LYNCH

FRANÇOIS TRUFFAUT JULES ET JIM

DOUGLAS HARDING

E. E. CUMMINGS

ALBERT CAMUS

COLIN WILSON THE OUTSIDER

JEAN-LUC GODARD HIROSHIMA MON AMOUR

JOHN STEINBECK THE PEARL

STEVE KILBEY

JOY DIVISION

ALAN GARNER

JOHN MARTYN

CHARLES BUKOWSKI

PART 5

PHOTOGRAPHS

PHOTO 1

A hand detector used for finding other children's
hands : 'Please find Zane's hand' - message
writing with purpose and authenticity.

PHOTO 2

Cuddling in with my brother about to co-adventure
into the world of Story - books open up new worlds
and the curling of my toes suggests that I
liked what I discovered !

PHOTO 3

The Spiral – the adventure through life, going with its flow. Courage in the face of malevolence and a strong sense of self are critical for the journey.

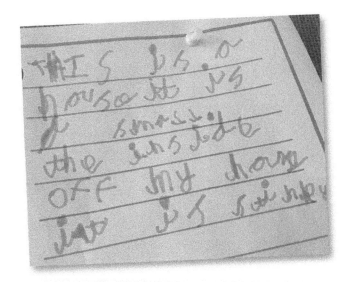

PHOTO 4

"This is my house it is small, the inside off my house is stinky." Drawing Club begins with secret symbols but because your 3Muing works at the cusp of skills, children grow in confidence ~~comprehension~~ – writing becomes something they know they can do.

PHOTO 5

Negotiating and solidarity prior to tyre building - planning isn't fixed for children, they are often the ultimate multi-taskers with each child acknowledging the ideas and strategies of one another.

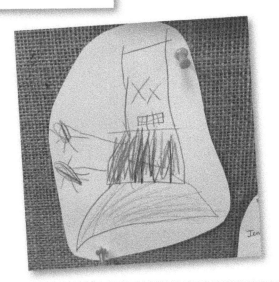

PHOTO 6

Independent robot illustration by a girl who five weeks previously had very little fine motor skill - she also counted the robot fingers on each hand before adding them together

PHOTO 7

The 3Ms is individualised with this child
writing 'come' and 'play' very early on in the
Autumn Term because she could + wanted
to use them. She also showed less confident
writers letter formation below - skills rubbing
off to each other.

PHOTO 8

Mathematics in play - recording secret
numbers for a passcode. Children talked about
numeral formation + supported one another
challenging themselves to write bigger numbers
in order.

PHOTO 9

From stick men to this witch drawing
as part of a Play Project in four weeks.
The details were modelled in Drawing Club
some weeks before although not the
cigarette or the feet inside those pointy
boots!

PHOTO 10

Pencil grip with confidence is a common
outcome of Drawing Club - this boy could
not hold a pencil unless it was in his
palm six weeks previously...

PHOTO 11

Giving children independence is critical,
not just to play but also to be part
of a team - this sense of belonging
is important if children are to work
democratically + for one another.

PHOTO 12

The Seventh Sense in action: these large
pegs are being used as weights to prevent
the girl from floating away. "I drank some
potion and now I'm weightless!"
- 'weightless' was introduced in Drama Club
two weeks previously.

PHOTO 13
Not all secret messages have to be symbols or writing. Often, children like to hide mini characters for others to find as part of paper-based small world play.

PHOTO 14
Pirate focused Play Project 'outcomes': fifteen pieces of treasure cut out and placed inside a treasure chest along with matching mineral, map, pirate ship illustrations and a secret message 'Captain Phillip's Chart'

PHOTO 15

Open ended parachute play enables children
to make dens and create games for
themselves - each child's ability and
physicality respected and accommodated.
Language development in waves through negotiation
and problem solving.

PHOTO 16

Fruit boxes are great for building with but
can also offer children opportunities to
make make for their own purposes. Here,
the children are drawing people for a
'box party' with one child with severe SEN
an active protagonist in play.

PHOTO 17

There's no better thing than when children 'see' maths : realising that two triangles can go together to make a square at the age of 3...

PHOTO 18-19

Self-reflection on drawings through shared wondering often leads to further details being added - buttons, pupils, ears, fingers, eyebrows and spots ("chicken pox")

PHOTO 18-19

Self-reflection on drawings through shared
wondering often leads to further details
being added – buttons, pupils, ears, fingers,
eyebrows and spots ("chicken pox")

PHOTO 20

Large scale provision maximises the
possibility for collaboration, language and
multiple co-existing play – factories are
a regular 'theme', where anything can
be made, all the while the resources to
choose from honing physical skills.

PHOTO 21

Sometimes Drawing Club is great to do on long pieces of wallpaper stretching across the room — used sparingly this can create a real buzz and its an effective way to use other muscles when lying down.

PHOTO 22

Independent Drawing Club can pop-up anywhere. The boy writing 'I can run to the bed!' had under-developed pencil grip fine weeks earlier. Exclamation marks were modelled holistically — no child's progress should be capped by Adult World pre-conceptions.

PHOTO 23 † 24

From palm grip to writing 'lamborghini' in
seven weeks - modelling advance vowel
diagraphs to all opens up wider possibilities:
phonics doesn't always have to be taught
on the carpet or linearly. Both boys
supported one another to find sounds

PHOTO 23 † 24

From palm grip to writing 'lamborghini' in
seven weeks - modelling advance vowel
diagraphs to all opens up wider possibilities:
phonics doesn't always have to be taught
on the carpet or linearly. Both boys
supported one another to find sounds

PHOTO 25

Being able to choose resources + interpret
them sends a clear message to children
about how we see them as capable +
creative - with no pre-determined
'doing-ness' children can immerse in
'being-ness.'

PHOTO 26

Cursive can be very dividing. Whatever your
school decides, if we are to avoid our
own stress, it's arguably better to be a positive
as you can - if you show you don't believe in
what children are being modelled then the
~~children~~ they will see g through you - deep
breath needed. From palm grip to sentence
writing in nine weeks...

PHOTO 27.

The timelessness of play and being lost
in the moment at hand. Construction for
self-chosen purpose can sometimes be
autonomous and not ~~reluctant~~ reliant on
collaboration - now and again, it's good
to get lost by yourself to find yourself.

PHOTO 28

~~Two boys 222 this~~ This developed from
an independent play, other children asking
to join in, extending a bridge into a
road stretching right round the room.
Children also hid secret messages under
the blocks as a 'trick'.

PHOTO 29.

Drawing Club is great for mathematics too - these zombies + their pet bat are eating numbers 'bigger than 12'

PHOTO 30

Investigation and discovery are real drivers behind play. Making sense and exploration leads children to experiment with 'why' and 'how' revealing higher order thinking if we stand back + wait for children to unfold themselves.

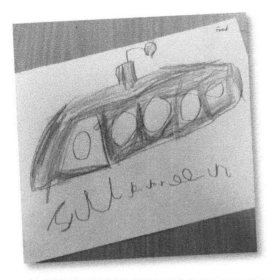

PHOTO 31

Joy + confidence shape writers who are
eager to create their own Drawing Club.
Writing 'submarine' in Week 7 of
Autumn Term

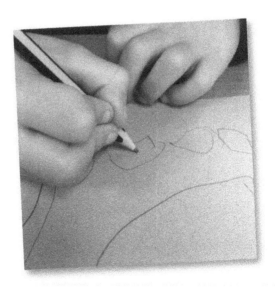

PHOTO 32

Children listen to other children. Modelling
pencil grip to one another - a confident
child to a child with delay, with no
adult influence - respect and love only.

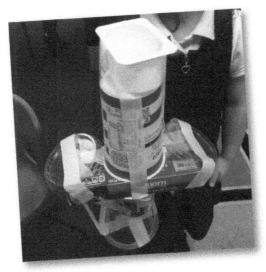

PHOTO 33

True creativity comes from the soul. It's not imitation of adult expectations. Anything can be any thing - a submarine with a zombie detector...

PHOTO 34

The Message Centre creates a culture that messaging is 'part of play - over time, children begin to see that messaging is for their purpose and use - they can message 'at will'.

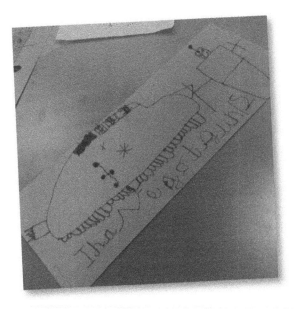

PHOTO 35

Drawing Club exploring 'Wacky Races' -
children designing new vehicles + their
special features - the level of detail
+ sentence coming independently from the
child.

PHOTO 36

The simplicity of the Seventh Sense: discus
equipment re-imagined as hairdressers
straighteners accompanied by child chat,
respect and turn-taking.

PHOTO 37
A cider factory in full flow - negotiation,
re-interpretation, shared thinking,
problem solving and oceans of language.
No adult needed...

PHOTO 38
Creativity at its finest. I've no idea
of the 'what' or 'why' but for the children
who spent over an hour on this, it was
important. Sometimes a mystery is best
left a mystery...

PHOTO 39

The author...

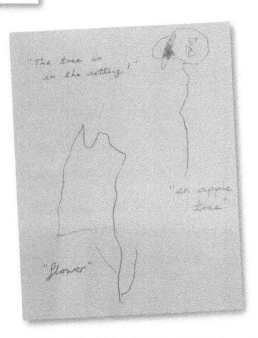

"The tree is in the setting!"

"an apple tree"

"flower"

PHOTO 40 + 41

In nine weeks of Drawing Club...

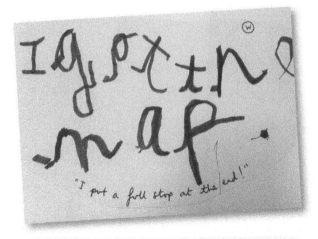

"I put a full stop at the end!"

PHOTO 40 + 41

In nine weeks of Drawing Club...

PHOTO 42

Collaborative games taking turns to throw balls into a lobster pot while it is being dragged. Physical development, mathematics and social interplay through the Seventh Sense...

Photo 43

Deconstructing the familiar can spark wonder in a whole new way. Taking apart old laptops reveals the 'small world' of electronics with all its 'what' 'how' and 'why!..,

Photo 44.

Joining in with children's play can go one of two ways. Thinking like a child can ~~make it go~~ increase the likelihood of it being positive. Children were rolling balls along a 20-metre section of ramp to land on ~~letters~~ numbers - the introduction of bigger numbers + 'poo bag' added an extra layer of engagement + 8Miy.

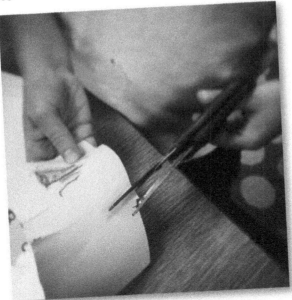

Week 45.
Children are quite capable of challenging
themselves + they can be creative about
it too!

~~Week~~ Photo 46
Drawing Club opens up the world of Story-
~~#####~~ one big imitation to adventure.

PHOTO 47

Play Projects often evolve into collaborative play, children drawn to one another skills + imagination - joint trial + error with all its encouragement + discovery leads children to know they belong.

PHOTO 48.

Drawing Club loves maps - they lend themselves to detail + are often part of children's play because they see the purpose + they can be hidden too!

PHOTO 49.

Pencil grip evolves ~~through~~ in Drawing Club
through modelling + emotional connection –
subtle physical development since
children aren't explicitly aware that this
is a by-product!

PHOTO 50 + 51

Play Projects aren't about 'having to do'.
They are a framework in which children
end up 3Ming themselves + one another

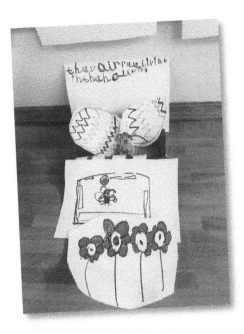

PHOTO 50 + 51

Play Projects aren't about 'having to do'.
They are a framework in which children
end up 3Ming themselves + one another

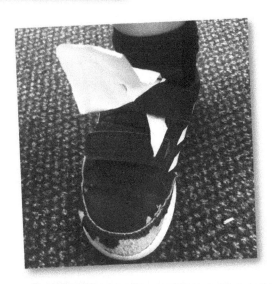

PHOTO 52

Secret messages can be hidden anywhere.
Velcro was born for secret messages +
the best bit is that they often go
home to be shared + to be wondered
about.

PHOTO 53

Children are capable. Every day they show us a magic door. We just need the faith to step through it.

INDEX